SUBVERSIVE OBEDIENCE

Subversive Obedience

WALTER BRUEGGEMANN

Edited by K. C. Hanson

scm press

© Walter Brueggemann 2011

Published in the UK in 2011 by SCM Press
Editorial office
13–17 Long Lane,
London, EC1A 9PN, UK

SCM Press is an imprint of Hymns Ancient & Modern Ltd
(a registered charity)
13A Hellesdon Park Road, Norwich,
Norfolk, NR6 5DR, UK

www.scmpress.co.uk

Published in the United States in 2011 as *Truth-Telling as Subversive
Obedience* by Cascade Books, An Imprint of Wipf&Stock Publishers,
199 W. 8th Ave., Suite 3, Eugene, OR 97401-2960

British Library Cataloguing in Publication data

A catalogue record for this book is available
from the British Library

978 0 334 04494 9

Printed and bound by
CPI Antony Rowe, Chippenham, Wiltshire

For John Buchanan

Contents

Foreword

THE BIBLICAL TEXT IS amazing, demanding, and frustratingly complex. And the challenge for any interpreter is to dig deep and explore the text—in all its diversity—in a fresh way. It has long been a joy of mine to read Walter Brueggemann's monographs, commentaries, essays, articles, sermons, and prayers because they always surprise and challenge me. That is why I assigned his works to my students and discuss them with colleagues. He does not look for easy answers. He does not look for a comfortable hermeneutic. What he does so well is listen to the text and interact with it in creativity. And his writing draws the readers in to listen for themselves what this text has to say. That is the hard work of interpretation.

This is the first volume of a series collecting Brueggemann's articles selected from *Journal of Preachers*, a periodical for which he is one of the editors. I hope you will share my sense of excitement in having new essays from him by which to be drawn into the text.

K. C. Hanson
Eugene, Oregon

Preface

WE HAVE KNOWN FOREVER that the truth (*nicht Arbeit!*) makes free (John 8:323). We have known it from the witness of Jesus, but not only from the witness of Jesus. We have known it in the hard work of personal and interpersonal relationships when at last, in the therapeutic process, we blurt out the truth that let us begin again. We have seen that emancipatory reality surging amid tyrannical governments when the truth of power and pain is spills into the streets, old patterns off control come unglued and new freedom becomes the order of the day.

Given that reality that we know very well, we have nonetheless an endless capacity—since the originary serpent—for deception and self-deception. We have, from Karl Marx, learned about the force of false consciousness that stalks us through propaganda and ideology until that "official truth" arrives at a trusted consensus. We have learned, from D. W. Winnicott, about "false selves" in which we cover over the true self in self-protective deception. We know, from Michel Foucault, about the alliance of power and truth and the Golden Rule whereby the ones with gold make the rules; and beyond the rules, the ones with power make the "world" we readily inhabit.

In our world of deception and self-deception and collusion, we ask in bewilderment with Pilate, "What is truth?" We yearn for truth, even while we cover our ears lest the truth be uttered in our presence. Because given enough of falseness to which we become inured, the utterance of truth is grossly unwelcome among us. As a consequence I believe, we live, all of us, on a precarious edge with our yearning and our fearfulness that our falsely constructed worlds will be interrupted and come tumbling down in chaos.

Into that world, we confess, has surged the God of the burning bush who turned out to be the God of the Exodus deliverance who turned out to be the God of the Sinai covenant. That God, so we are told, was attracted by the voiced pain of enslaved Israel, and so took on the false world of Pharaoh. And beyond that, at Sinai this same God declared the charter of neighborliness as an alternative to Pharaoh's quota-driven phoniness. And since that time, from that utterance at Sinai, God's people have been struggling with the dilemma of the demands of Pharaoh who holds all the visible power and the option of covenantal obedience. Given the sequence of Exodus-Sinai, we find this God to be the God of all truth.

But there is more than that in this strange narrative. After the deal is sealed at Sinai and Israel has sworn to obey this new emancipatory truth, Moses must still speak. In the form of demanding petition, Moses dares to speak truth to Yahweh, now and again talking Yahweh out of Yahweh's self-protective resolve. And since those exchanges, truth of a covenantal kind has consisted in an interpretive back-and-forth between the God of all truth and the bold characters who carry pain and hope to the throne of truth.

It does not surprise that Jesus, child of this back-and-forth tradition, stands before the Roman governor—or the Roman governor stands before Jesus—to probe truth (John 18:38). Of course the governor, agent of the state, trusts the truth that he knows and represents. He has relied on his authority until he stands before Jesus who exposes all "established truth" as false. That confrontation is an epitome of the crisis that Jesus characteristically evokes in the world, because his presence is truth-telling and his vocation breaks the pattern of deception and self-deception to make way for new life. It turns out, of course as Elisabeth Schüssler-Fiorenza has seen, that even this Jesus who is the truth (as well as the way and the life) must, in the Synoptic tradition, still have truth spoken to him. And so this uncredentialed woman must instruct Jesus to move out of his tribal containment in daring ways: "But she answered him . . ." (Mark 7:28). Thus even with Jesus who is "the truth," there is evidence that the matter is not one of certitude, but one of dialogical engagement of a most serious and transformative kind.

The contest between false consciousness, false self, and false worlds and the offer of truth is an old and on-going one. It is as old as Moses and Pharaoh, as on-going as Jesus and Pilate, and as demanding as present circumstance among us. We now have abundance of false worlds constructed by the feeding frenzy of consumerism and by the national passion for exceptionalism (chosenness) that in turn feeds military adventurism and economic expansionism. We now have the phoniness of narrow moralism and the reaction of unbridled individualism. We now have a powerful ideological claim that contains us all in a rush totalism that will not countenance anything outside of it or to the contrary. The force of that ideology has compelling and coercive ways to punish those who say or act otherwise.

But of course the truth must be spoken, for our lives depend on it, truth that subverts our best self-deceiving certitudes. The church has no monopoly on this vocation of truth-telling. But it is nonetheless the emancipatory vocation of the church. And that vocation, as before Pharaoh and as before the Roman governor, is not welcome. It is unwelcome because the freedom it generates is scary, rather like living without a safety net. There are other voices of truth-telling as well; but the church is peculiarly defined by that task. And those who serve as truth-tellers in the church, like those who listen to the truth-telling in the church, are a mix of yearning and fearfulness, of receptiveness and collusion. In the end, the work of truth-telling is not to offer a new package of certitudes that displaces old certitudes. This truth to be uttered and acted, rather, is the enactment and conveyance of this Person who is truth, so that truth comes as bodily fidelity that stays reliably present to the pain of the world. Since the old Exodus, the truth has emerged in unexpected ways, from below. As an alternative to the alliance of power and truth that Foucault has so well chronicled, this evangelical offer of truth arises in a convergence of holy resolve and voiced pain, a convergence made echoingly available in the cry from the cross where human pain and divine purpose intersect.

↶

The *Journal of Preachers*, from which these several pieces are reprinted in revised form, continues to play a modest but significant role in energizing, enlightening, and empowering preachers who take seriously the hard, ambiguous work of truth-telling that subverts the deathliness of our many deceptions. The *Journal* regularly features preachers who are themselves constantly at that dangerous task, even while they preside over and administer institutions that require programmatic support. The *Journal,* moreover, is a meeting place for many readers who continue this glorious work of subversion. I am privileged to be connected to the *Journal* and am greatly indebted to our editor, Erskine Clarke, for his long-term friendship, his wisdom and tenacity about what the *Journal* is to do, and not least for his permission to reprint these pieces. I also express my thanks and appreciation to his various assistants in the grunt work of the *Journal,* including Betty Cousar, Jet Harper, and Rosemary Raynal. As always, I am grateful to K. C. Hanson, along with his associates at Wipf and Stock. I rely on K. C. for his continuing generative, imaginative work that turns more-or-less random thoughts into readable material.

I am glad to dedicate this little book with thanks to John Buchanan at the moment he moves toward retirement. Over many years John has been a force and a reference point for courageous, reliable, steadfast truthfulness. The prospect of his continuing work in other venues will keep many of us from losing heart. John knows, of course, that preaching is sheer foolishness; he knows as well that it is utterly important for our freed future, and for that reason must be done as well and as carefully, and as daringly as he has tried to do.

Walter Brueggemann
Columbia Theological Seminary
Easter season 2011

1

Duty as Delight and Desire

WE MAY AS WELL concede at the outset that we live, all of us, in a promiscuous, self-indulgent society that prizes autonomy.[1] As a consequence, "obedience" is a tough notion, which we settle mostly either by the vaguest of generalizations, or by confining subject matter to those areas already agreed upon.

Two Dimensions of the Problem

The fearfulness and avoidance of obedience, as conventionally understood among us, has in my judgment two root causes, both of which are alive and powerful, even though not often frontally articulated.

The first dimension of the problem is the Augustinian-Lutheran dichotomy of "grace and law," which runs very deep in Western theology. In his treatment of Paul, Augustine considerably upped the stakes of the issue in his crushing opposition to Pelagius, and Luther solidified that theological claim by boldly inserting

---

1. McHugh helpfully speaks of "cultural antinomianism" and explores its costliness for society: "Psychiatric Misadventures," 192. The best series of case studies for this condition is offered by Bellah et al, *Habits of the Heart*.

1

the word "alone" in his reading of Paul, thus "grace *alone*." It is clear that by "law" Luther meant many different things, seemingly focused especially on life apart from the gospel. The result, however, has been a remarkable aversion to "works," as though obedience to the commands of God, that is, performances of "works," is in and of itself a denial of the gospel. Luther is of course much more subtle and knowing than this, but he has thus been conventionally interpreted. The outcome has been a notion of gospel without demand, a notion that plays well in a "therapeutic" society.

An aspect of this strong dichotomy has been a latent but pervasive anti-Jewish stereotype. Thus "law" is easily assigned to the "Jews," and the Old Testament becomes a book of commandments that has been "superseded" by the free gospel of Christ. Such a common maneuver of course fails to understand the core dynamic of covenantal faith shared by Jews and Christians, and inevitably feeds anti-Semitism.[2] It is sufficient here simply to observe that such a reading of the gospel of Paul, powerfully reinforced by a sustained German-Lutheran reading of Romans, is at least open to question. Krister Stendahl has proposed that Augustine and Luther have massively misread Paul, who is concerned not with "guilt," but with Jewish-Christian relations in the early church.[3] And E. P. Sanders has contributed greatly to the exposition of Stendahl's proposal, so that this governing dichotomy needs to be seriously challenged and reconsidered.[4] The task of such reconsideration is a difficult one, given the force of these old categories.

The second dimension of our problem is the Enlightenment notion of unfettered freedom of "Man Come of Age." Indeed, the central program of the Enlightenment has been to slough off any larger authority to which obedience is owed, and that with special

2. Van Buren has explored a healthier understanding of the matter of torah shared by Christians and Jews: *A Theology of the Jewish Christian Reality, Part 2: A Christian Theology of the People Israel*, 158–59 and passim.

3. Stendahl, "The Apostle Paul and the Introspective Conscience of the West."

4. Among his important works on the subject, see Sanders, *Paul and Palestinian Judaism*. See his several discussions in the book of "covenantal nomism."

reference to the traditional authority of the church.[5] This notion of freedom is already rooted in Descartes's establishment of the *human* doubter as the norm of truth. Locke contributed to the cause with his notion of the human person as a rational, free decider, and Kant completed the "Turn Toward the Subject," in making the human autonomous actor the one who will shape functional reality. This Enlightenment ideology has received its popular form in a Freudian theory of repression in which human maturation is the process of emancipation from communal authority that is extrinsic to the individual person and therefore fundamentally alien to mature humanness. Thus the human goal is movement beyond any restraints that come under the category of repression.

It turns out, of course, that such a model of unfettered freedom is an unreachable mirage. The individual person is never so contextless, and in the end the fantasy of such freedom has culminated in the most choking of conformities.[6] There is, to be sure, an element of truth in Enlightenment models of liberation, but such a notion is almost always insufficiently dialectical to bear upon the actual human situation.

These theological-theoretical matters may seem quite remote from the concrete task of "preaching obedience." In my judgment, however, pastor and congregation must engage these powerful (even if hidden) categories and assumptions in critical and knowing ways, in order to face the commands of God honestly. The reason they must be faced is that they are concretely powerful, even if mostly unarticulated. It is false to take the "law/grace" dichotomy at face value, as though the creator of heaven and earth has no overriding, non-negotiable intention for God's creatures. It is equally false to accept the phoney freedom of autonomy, and find ourselves more deeply enmeshed in the commands of death.

5. For a classic discussion of the issues of the Enlightenment vis-à-vis the traditional authority of the church, see Hazard, *The European Mind, 1680–1715.*

6. On the production of conformity and homogeneity by the Enlightenment, see Gunton, *Enlightenment & Alienation: An Essay Towards a Trinitarian Theology*; and his more recent work, *The One, The Three, and The Many: God, Creation, and the Culture of Modernity.*

3

Only the exposure of these false articulations can permit the community of the gospel to discern and accept its true position before God, who loves, delivers, summons, and commands.[7]

Conditional Relationships

A rereading of the gospel of grace and a reconsideration of Enlightenment ideology, in my judgment, will lead to a stunning and compelling fresh awareness: our most serious relationships, including our relationship to the God of the gospel, are, at the same time, *profoundly unconditional* and *massively conditional.* One can, I submit, test this odd claim, both in terms of our normative theological materials and in terms of our lived experience. Such a notion of course violates all of our either/or Aristotelian logic, but our most treasured relations are not subject to such an exclusionary logic.

Much Old Testament scholarship (including some of my own) has championed the notion that there are two traditions of covenant in the Old Testament, one unconditional (Abraham and David) and one conditional (Moses).[8] While this is critically correct, our theological task is to try to understand these textual claims taken all together.[9] The evidence to which I am drawn suggests in powerful ways that "conditional/unconditional" and "law/grace" are unworkable categories for understanding our most serious and treasured relationships. And these misguided polarities create great crises for understanding the odd dialectical character of the gospel.

---

7. Fackenheim has shown how the dialectic of "saving and commanding" asserts the primal work of God with Israel (*God's Presence in History*).

8. The clearest, most direct statement of this tension is that of Freedman, "Divine Commitment and Human Obligation The Covenant Theme"; Levenson has written a programmatic rebuttal of the antithesis commonly assumed in scholarship (*Sinai and Zion: An Entry Into the Jewish Bible*).

9. See the exposition of Childs, *Biblical Theology of the Old and New Testaments*, 532–65; and Childs, *Old Testament Theology in a Canonical Context*, 51–83.

We may take as emblematic of such relationships that are neither conditional nor unconditional, as does the Old Testament texts, the relations of husband-wife and parent-child. In either of these at its best, it is clear that the relationship is unconditional, that is, there is no circumstance under which the relationship will be voided. And yet in these very same relationships, there are high and insistent "expectations" of the other which shade over into demands.[10] And when these expectations are not met, there may be woundedness, alienation, or even rejection, even though the wounded party is powerfully committed.[11] The truth is that there is something inscrutable about such relationships that are both conditional and unconditional; or perhaps we should say neither unconditional nor conditional. If one seeks to make one term or the other final in characterizing such a relationship, we destroy the inscrutability that belongs to and defines the relationship.[12]

10. Wrong has written suggestively about the authority of expectation, though he is concerned for political theory and not theological force: *The Problem of Order: What Unites and Divides Society*, 42–58. He writes:

> The ambiguity of expectation becomes apparent only when we consider its use m communications such as that of a mother telling her child that she "expects" obedience at school to the teacher, or of the admiral addressing the fleet who affirms that "England expects every man to do his duty."
>
> The mother and the admiral are not simply predicting out loud future events or common interest their utterances to the child and to the assembled fleet are m the imperative mode the expectations asserted are intended to bring about the conduct they claim to be anticipating The child, after all, knows, and the mother knows the child knows, that disobedience at school will be reported at home and lead to possibly unpleasant results.
>
> Expectations may, I have argued, function as imperatives, as normative demands constraining the human objects of expectation to conform to them The emergence of expectations-cum-norms out of recurrent interaction is a process that goes on all the time, if often in trivial and evanescent ways. (42–43, 46, 51)

11. Notice that often the "sanction" is not articulated but is inherent in the expectation itself, because of the authority of the one who expects.

12. This seems to be recognized even in popular ways, so that the attempt at "unconditional" finally requires some conditionally See the belated

It may indeed be regarded as a far leap from our experience with such relationships as husband-wife and parent-child to our relation with God. It is of course a leap made artistically and boldly in the text itself. It will, moreover, be objected that one cannot reason by analogy or metaphor about God, and yet it is the only language we have for this most serious and freighted of all relationships. Moreover, we must ask why the poets of ancient Israel chose to speak this way about God. I suggest that such images are utilized because the poets who have given us our primal language for God are seeking a way to voice an inscrutability that overrides our logic and is more like the inscrutability of serious relationships than it is like anything else.[13]

The covenant God has with us, with Israel, with the world, is a command-premised relation. The covenant is based in command, and God expects to be obeyed.[14] There are, moreover, sanctions and consequences of disobedience that cannot be avoided, even as there are gifts and joys along with obedience.[15] The torah is given for guidance, so that Israel (and all of Israel's belated heirs) are "clued in" to the defining expectations of this relationship. The torah makes clear that the holy "Other" in this relationship is an Agent with will and purpose that must be taken seriously and cannot be disregarded or mocked.

Thus it is a *covenantal relation* which is the "underneath category" to which "grace and law," "conditional and unconditional"

---

discovery of this in Masters and Johnson, *The Pleasure Bond*; and the analysis of Yankelovitch, *New Rules: Searching for Self-Fulfillment in a World Turned Upside Down*.

13. This is a point at which Karl Barth's resistance of the *analogia entis* (analogy of being) and his embrace of *analogia fidei* (the analogy of faith) might be considered. Eberhard Busch places Barth's concerns in context: *Karl Barth: His Life from Letters and Autobiographical Texts*, 215–16 and passim.

14. Kutsch goes so far as to suggest that "covenant" (*berith*) in fact means "obligation": "Gesetz und Gnade Probleme des alttestamentlichen Bundesbegriffs."

15. Mendenhall made the case that "sanctions" belong to the structure and substance of covenant: *Law and Covenant in Israel and the Ancient Near East*. More generally, see the discussion of Wrong, *Problem of Order*, on the reality of sanctions in social relations.

are subsets.[16] The "Other" in this relation is a real, live Other who initiates, shapes, watches over, and cares about the relation. The "Other" is both *mutual* with us and *incommensurate* with us, in a way not unlike a parent is mutual and incommensurate with a child, or a teacher is mutual and incommensurate with a student. This means that the relation is endlessly open, alive, giving and demanding, and at risk. This Holy Other may on occasion act in stunning mutuality, being with and for the second party, and so draw close in mercy and compassion, in suffering and forgiveness. It is, however, this same God who may exhibit God's self in un-accommodating incommensurability with rigorous expectation and dreadfulness, when expectations are not met. It is our desperate effort to reduce or "solve" the wonder of "the Holy one in our midst" that leads to such distortions as law and grace, freedom and servitude, unconditional and conditional.[17] No such pairing can adequately contain the inscrutability, liveliness, danger, and unsettled quality of this relationship. Israel thus knows that torah is *guidance,* in order to be joyously "on the way," a way that constitutes the well-being of the relationship.[18]

Two Interpretive Strategies

This core insight about the richness of a covenantal relation still leaves for the preacher and the congregation the demanding work of taking seriously the specific commands of this covenantal "Other." Clearly the commands and guidance of the God of Israel and of the church are not vague and fuzzy, but quite concrete in how they concern the specificities of life. Those bound with this God are summoned to act differently in every sphere of life. Indeed,

16. "Covenantal nomism" (on which see Sanders, *Paul and Palestinian Judaism*) nicely juxtaposes terms that articulate the subtle dimensions of covenant as a *relation* and as *demand*.

17. On this phrase, see the old but reliable discussion of Eichrodt, "The Holy One in Your Midst: The Theology of Hosea."

18. On "the way" as a governing image for Israel's life of obedient faith, see Muilenburg, *The Way of Israel Biblical Faith and Ethics*; and Van Buren, *Discerning the Way*.

obedience consists in bringing every zone of our existence under the will, purpose, and expectation of this covenantal partner. While the concrete enactments of these commands in almost every case face ambiguity and complexity,[19] the most crucial issue for reflection and preaching is to frame the commands so that they are not alien impositions, extrinsic to our life, but belong to and are embraced as definitional for the very fabric of our existence.[20]

For that purpose, I suggest two possible interpretive strategies. The first is that the commands of God are the *disciplines essential to the revolution* that is Yahwism.[21] Every serious revolutionary movement requires exacting disciplines of its adherents. And while the requirements may vary, they all in substance concern single-minded devotion to the revolution, without any doubt, ambiguity, or reservation. A revolution has no chance of success unless all of its adherents are singularly committed to the vision and the project, and are willing to play their assigned role with unquestioning reliability and responsiveness.

The revolution to which the biblical community is summoned is to enact in the world of social affairs a new practice of social relationships marked by justice, mercy, and peace, which touches all of life. In order to engage in such a practice, all those committed to this revolutionary vision are expected to enact the daily requirements concerning self toward God, and self toward neighbor, in order to "advance the revolution."

---

19. Concerning the ambiguity and complexity of the commandments that require ongoing interpretation, see Brueggemann, "The Commandments and Liberated, Liberating Bonding," chapter 5 below.

20. I understand legalism to refer to commands that are imposed but not gladly received and embraced as one's own. The model of Job's friends is the standard example m the Bible. Such imposition tends to be rigid and coercive, without taking into account the impact of context or experience. On this matter as it relates to freedom and health, see Bollas, *The Shadow of the Object*, 135–56, and his notion of a "normatic personality."

21. More than anyone else, Gottwald has shown the ways m which Israel is revolutionary in terms of its social intention: *The Tribes of Yahweh*, 489–92 and passim. Gottwald's articulation is enormously valuable, even if one does not follow all of his socio-historical analysis.

Or to change the figure slightly, Jesus and his disciples, that is, the ones under his discipline, are "on the way" as the "Kingdom of God draws near," a kingdom in which the "normalcies" of life are turned on their head. The disciples are variously summoned and dispatched, to order their lives around "prayer and fasting," around empty-handed healing power, to live their lives as concrete testimony that the new realm is "at hand," and can be lived and practiced here and now.

In order to make this approach to "obedience" convincing, believers must come to see their baptism as entry into a new vision of reality, which carries with it all sorts of new possibilities that the world thinks impossible.[22] This vision of reality is an oddity in the world, at odds with all the conventional orderings of society, political, economic, and social. This "signing on" is not an "extra" added to a normal life, but entails a reordering of all of one's life from the ground up. The specificities of obedience must constantly be seen as derivative from and in the service of the larger revolution. It is clear that Moses imagined a whole new way of being in the world, a way ordered as covenant, and the commands of Sinai provide the guidance for that new way. And in like fashion, it is clear that the movement around Jesus evoked such hostility and resistance, precisely because his movement subverted all conventional practices and forms in the world. No doubt such demands and disciplines became "legalistic" when the concrete requirement was no longer understood to derive from a larger revolutionary intention.

I am aware that such a notion of "revolutionary discipline" will not be easily compelling for most of us in excessively complacent establishment Christianity. I do imagine, however, that for many persons (especially young people), such a notion may indeed be a powerful attraction, for it is an enactment of a powerful hope for newness midst an increasingly failed and despairing society.

In any case, I suggest a second strategy for "preaching obedience." It is this: believers are those who love God with their whole heart, or more colloquially for Christians, "love the Lord Jesus."

Such "love" is to be understood in all its rich implication, both as *agape* and *eros,* as true heart's desire.[23] This is imagery not often utilized in our Calvinist inheritance, beset as we are with a heavy sense of duty. But alongside *duty,* in any serious relationship are *desire* and *delight,* the energetic will to be with the one loved, to please the one loved, to find in the joy of the one loved, one's own true joy. Thus one in love is constantly asking in the most exaggerated way, what else can I do in order to delight the beloved? In such a context, one does not count the cost, but anticipates that when the beloved is moved in joy, it will be one's own true joy as well. Indeed, in such a condition, one can find joy only in the joy of the beloved, and not apart from the joy of the beloved.

Thus the psalmist can speak of such true heart's desire:

> One thing I asked of Yahweh,
>> that I will seek after:
> to live in the house of Yahweh
>> all the days of my life,
> to behold the beauty of Yahweh,
>> and to inquire in his temple. (Ps 27:4)

> Whom have I in heaven but you?
>> And there is nothing on earth that I desire other than you.
> (Ps 73:25)

Of the last verse, Calvin comments:

23. It will be recognized that my approach here flies in the face of the classic arguments of Nygren, *Agape and Eros.* I do this with considerable diffidence, because I am thoroughly schooled in Nygren's argument. I have come to think, however, that Nygren imposed categories that may have been required in his context, but that in doing so, he overlooked dimensions of the ethic of Israel and the church that moved beyond duty to the embrace of joy in faith. For our purposes, Nygren's discussion of Augustine (449–563) is especially important.

I should also mention that Moran has shown that in some cases in the ancient Near East, "love" is a political word bespeaking acknowledgment of sovereignty: "The Ancient Near Eastern Background of the Love of God in Deuteronomy."

> I know that thou by thyself, apart from every other object,
> art sufficient, yea, more than sufficient for me, and there-
> fore I do not suffer myself to be carried away after a vari-
> ety of desires, but rest in and am fully contented with thee.
> In short, that we may be satisfied with God alone, it is of
> importance for us to know the plentitude of the blessings
> which he offers for our acceptance.[24]

The true believer desires most of all being with the beloved.

None has understood this as well or as eloquently as Augustine, who saw that the most elemental craving of our life is communion with God. He begins his *Confessions* with the well-known affirmation:

> Thou awakest us to delight in Thy praise;
>
> > for Thou madest us for Thyself,
>
> and our heart is restless,
>
> > until it repose in Thee.[25]

And in his subsequent comment, he adds, "Thou also gavest me to desire no more than Thou gavest."[26] This sense of keen desire, not

24. John Calvin, *Commentary on the Book of Psalms, Volume Second* (Grand Rapids: Baker, 1979), 155. It should be noted, however, that Calvin still resists the notion of the intrinsic satisfaction of the relationship, and must appeal to "the plentitude of blessing" that seem extrinsic to the relation of communion itself.

25. Augustine, *The Confession of St Augustine, Bishop of Hippo*, 1.

26. Ibid., 5. Special attention should be given to the recent study of *The Confessions* by Margaret R. Miles, *Desire and Delight: A New Reading of Augustine's Confessions*. Against the grain of the argument of Nygren, Miles proposes that the *Confessions* are intended by Augustine to be a "text of pleasure," and that the pleasure of the reader is linked to Augustine's own struggle for pleasure His argument is that he tried every pleasure the world could offer and only finds his true desire in communion with God. This is not a stifling of desire but the proper focus on the desire which is appropriate to the human heart. Miles summarizes her argument:

> The *Confessions* is, among other things, a narrative deconstruction
> of what is ordinarily thought of as pleasurable, and a reconstruction
> of "true" pleasure. He was quite clear about what constituted the
> condition of greatest pleasure by the time he wrote the *Confessions*

without its erotic dimension, is echoed in Bach's sterner notion of Jesus as the "joy of man's desiring." Thus "obedience" is a concrete, visible way of enacting and entering that desire, so that duty converges completely with the desire and delight of communion. It is not that obedience is instrumental and makes communion possible, but obedience itself is a mode of "being with" the desired in joy, delight, and well-being. In a quite concrete way, it is profoundly satisfying to do what the beloved most delights in.

Now I imagine that like "disciplines for revolution," the notion of "the desire of the beloved" will not be easy in the starchier traditions of Christian faith. Our more preferred strategy has been to renounce desire and focus on duty, on the affirmation that desire per se is an ignoble enterprise. This way of understanding obedience in relation to desire, however, honors the reality that we are indeed desiring creatures. God has made us so, and so we are. The work of obedience then, is not to squelch desire or deny it, as some modes of piety are wont to do, for then denied desire breaks out in destructive ways. Our work rather is to critique distorted desire and refocus desire on the true and faithful subject of our proper delight and longing. The intention of consumerism and its ideology of advertising is to distort and misdirect desire, as though the foundational desire of our life is for shoes, deodorant, beer, a car, or the best detergent. At the core of our creatureliness, however, such desires are fundamentally irrelevant. That is not what we want of life and they do not satisfy.

---

(20). The pleasure experiment has come to a dead end (32). The key to pleasure, for Augustine, was ideally not the sacrifice of some pleasures so that others could be cultivated. It was the ordering of all the pleasures of a human life so that those associated with enjoyment of objects m the sensible world would not usurp all of a person's attention and affection When pleasures are constellated around a single object of love, he said, they can be enjoyed without fear of distraction (37). Augustine learned more than he acknowledged from sex, that he learned "the deep and irreplaceable knowledge of [his] capacity for joy" from his sexual experience, and that it was precisely *this* experimental knowledge from which Augustine extrapolated his model of spiritual pleasure (71).

Faith confesses that it is none other than the very creator of heaven and earth who constitutes our true desire, so that only when our hearts rest in God can our restlessness be ended and satisfied. Thus the commandments are specific strategies for redirecting and reaffirming legitimate desire, not in any way a denial of desire, but in full affirmation of true desire. Thus God is the one for whom we seek, "as the deer longs for flowing streams" (Ps 42:1). The metaphor suggests, according to the older translations, that the faithful "pant for" God and must have God for the wholeness of life. It is no wonder that obedience is a joy and delight, because it is an act in and of itself of communion with the one for whom we constantly and rightly yearn.

The Decalogue: Love of God and Neighbor

The core summons to obedience, that is, a) the core disciplines for the revolution, and b) the core practices of our true desire, are voiced in the Decalogue.[27] As is well known, the two "tablets" of the ten commands are focused on "love of God" and "love of neighbor." On these two enterprises "hang all the torah and the prophets." Such a simple prospectus for obedience comprehends enormous teaching material through which to invite the baptized to a new life of *revolutionary devotion* and *singleness of desire*.

The first four commands concerning "the love of God" reflect on the true subject of our life, the holy God who is our alpha and omega, the source and goal of all our life. This is the baseline for all biblical preaching and the primal claim of our faith. Our life consists in loving God for God's own sake. That is what we are created to do.[28]

27. On the Decalogue, see Harrelson, *The Ten Commandments and Human Rights*; Childs, *Old Testament Theology*, 63–83; Miller, *The Ten Commandments*; and Brown, ed., *The Ten Commandments*.

28. This is of course reminiscent of the classic answer of the Westminster Catechism, "Man's Chief Concern is to glorify God and enjoy him forever." It is striking that the second half of the sentence speaks of the "enjoyment of God," which is the satisfaction of desire that encompasses duty and moves beyond duty to delight.

How odd to yearn toward God! The commands in Exod 20:1–7 assert that the primal quality and character of Yahweh de-absolutize every other claim and loyalty, and invite the renunciation of every addictive loyalty, conservative or liberal, which drives our life toward restlessness and phoniness. Moreover, the commands show that God is an "end" and not a "means," has no utilitarian value, but is to be loved purely for God's own sake. Such an affirmation about God cuts against all calculating obedience. Long before Job, Moses understood that Israel is called to "serve God for nought" (Job 1:9), that is, to gain nothing but only to be in this lively relation of duty and delight. Imagine what would happen if the church talked honestly about de-absolutizing all our quarrelsome addictions of mind and heart which tend to make all sorts of things absolutes which draw our life into knotted stomachs, clenched fists, and stern speech![29]

The second tablet (Exod 20:8–17) asserts that the second true desire of our life, derivative from the first, is to have "good neighbors," that is, to live in a neighborhood. A true neighborhood is never a gift that floats down from the sky, but is wrought through the revolutionary work of obedience.[30] If we ever gain clarity about our true desire, it will quickly become evident to us that the yearning for good neighbors cannot be satisfied by any shoes, deodorant, beer, car, or detergent. They are not what we desire! And so our energy might be redirected toward neighborly matters like housing, education, health care, and away from coveting (Exod 20:17) and all the distortions of commandments five through nine which serve coveting (Exod 20:8–16). It is no wonder that the Decalogue is at the center of the Reformation catechisms, and that Luther and Calvin spent so much energy on it. Note well that when revolutionary vision and true desire are manifested, it becomes

---

29. A proviso is important that such a notion is not an invitation for the preacher to focus on his or her favorite causes or animosities My impression is that rightly done, the notion of critical obedience gives aid and comfort to no one, but challenges all of our pet modes of utilitarian obedience.

30. On this theme, see von Rad, "Brother and Neighbor in the Old Testament."

exceedingly difficult to be coercive and scolding about obedience. These commands are not primarily social restraints or modes of social control, but are about possibilities for life that emerge from "coming down where we ought to be." But conversely, when we have become ambivalent about the requirements of the revolution or caught in distorted desires, it is predictable that what begins as an offer of communion becomes coerciveness. And yet it is clear no amount of reproof can help people find their way into true communion by way of revolutionary passion or focused desire. Such passion and desire are not generated by strident insistence or ideological imposition.

Sexuality and Economics

It is only slightly reductive to say that the two great accents of Freud and Marx, sexuality and economics, are the two great arenas for evangelical obedience, and the two zones in which we decide about our devotion to the covenantal revolution and where we enact our true desire. It follows that sexuality and economics, zones of great power, are also the most likely candidates for distortion and loss of the very communion for which we so yearn.

Sexuality

Freud understood that sexuality is a sphere of endless inscrutability, the arena of our true selves and the place in our life for deepest deception and pathology. Thus obedience in sexuality is a primary agenda of evangelical faith, as is evident by the enormously destructive quarrels and high investment of energy in the church, after long centuries of repression, denomination, and exploitation.

It is relatively easy (and I think useless) for the church simply to champion a flat "sex ethic" of a quite traditional kind. That of course is one very live option in the church.[31] But if obedience in

31. Marva J. Dawn has shown in a fine study how a rather conventional sexual ethic is open to a much more dense significance: *Sexual Character: Beyond Technique to Intimacy*.

sexuality is to reflect and derive from (either or both) discipline for the revolution and/or a core desire for communion, then the categories of covenantal fidelity and covenantal freedom must be primary ingredients in our thinking and acting. Such a perspective requires much more than embracing traditional mores, because fidelity means something quite different from "abstaining" or "staying married" or "being straight." It means rather being in a relation that is genuinely life-giving and life-receiving, where the work of neighbor regard is practiced. And covenantal freedom means finding modes of fidelity congruent with one's true self and the capacity to be emancipated from "legal" relationships that are in fact destructive and hopelessly demeaning. Thus the specificity of obedience in sexuality may most often come down to a "set of workable conventions," but when that set of conventions is deeply coercive, it does not serve the covenantal revolution, and instead of focusing true desire, it likely crushes desire or misdirects it, so that one's true self is cut off from God and neighbor.[32]

Economics

Marx understood, conversely, that money is a sphere of endless inscrutability, an arena of our true selves, and a place in our life for deep deception and alienation. Obedience with money is a powerful agenda for evangelical faith, as is evident by the profound disagreements in the church about ways in which to think about the earning, saving, investing, sharing, and spending of money, and the relative merits of different economic systems and policies. The Bible, moreover, spends enormous amounts of space and energy on such issues.

It is relatively easy (and I think unhelpful) for the church to champion a traditional ethics of money that simply reflects the practices of society, whether in a market economy or a state

---

32. It cannot be said too often that after Israel (or we) arrive at workable rules, the rules endlessly require on-going interpretation, to take account of context, experience, and new learning This is inevitable, and we either do it knowingly or without recognizing that we are doing such interpretation.

economy. It is usual practice for the church in our U.S. context to embrace what is conventionally understood as "Protestant work ethic." It turns out, however, that such a "work ethic" is for our time and place inordinately simplistic, and fails to take into account the ambiguities and complexities of a global economic reality with astonishing disparities between "haves" and "have-nots."[33] Moreover, such an ethic does not seem to make such contact with those who are so affluent that they can create smaller zones of well-being which screen out the presence of the neighbor.[34] It seems increasingly clear that the culminating command of Moses, "Thou shalt not covet," now requires a carefully nuanced exposition that for affluent people moves well beyond such conventions as a "tithe," and addresses the systemically driven acquisitiveness of a consumer ethic in which neighbor questions have evaporated.[35]

As in sexuality, so in economics, covenantal obedience concerns the practice of covenantal fidelity and covenantal freedom, fidelity to see that all of our resources are held in trust in and for the neighbor with whom life is shared, and freedom that entails the practice of choices which attend both to the genuine regard of self and the genuine delight in generosity which enhances the neighborhood. True covenantal desire is not satisfied by acquisitiveness, even on a grand scale, but is satisfied only by the valuing of neighbor, even as self is valued. A reordered perception of obedience in economics is of enormous urgency for the covenantal revolution. It entails a repentance from false desire to which we have become blindly and uncritically committed.

It will be helpful, and in the end necessary, to see that obedience in sexuality and obedience in economics are of a piece. The interrelatedness of the two spheres of obedience exposes a

33. See the thoughtful discussion of the issues by Duchrow, *Global Economy: A Confessional Issue for the Churches.*

34. Galbraith, *The Culture of Contentment*, has written an acute study of this propensity in enclaves of wealth in our society.

35. Chaney has shown how the tenth commandment is concerned with policies and practices of systemic acquisitiveness: "You Shall Not Covet Your Neighbor's House."

profound contradiction in our common life in the U.S. It is conventional among us (and echoed by the more conservative voices of the church) to seek to impose puritanical restraint upon sexuality, all the while encouraging economic promiscuity for the sake of "economic growth."[36] It is not, however, a gain to reverse the process (with dissenting liberals in the church) to encourage economic transformation while being uncritically and thoughtlessly more open about liberty in sexuality. Either way, such disparity sends mixed signals and fails to maintain the delicacy of fidelity and freedom that belongs to covenantal relations.[37] Both coercive restraint and sanctioned promiscuity, whether in sexuality or in economics, violate the profound relatedness that belongs to evangelical obedience. It is clear, in my judgment, that the church must learn to speak differently about both spheres, in relation to each other, and in relation to the larger issues of genuine revolution and true desire.

Rethinking Faithful Obedience

It is my judgment that we live in a moment in the U.S. church that requires a serious and explicit rethinking of the meaning of faithful obedience. At the core of evangelical faith is the claim that faith knows some things that matter for genuine life, which are now urgent for our society. Such an explicit rethinking which is the work of the whole congregation may operate with these affirmations:

36. A classic example of this incongruity is the way in which Roman Catholics in this country are uncompromisingly zealous about the issue of abortion (and other matters of sexuality), but are largely indifferent to the wondrous Bishops' Letter on economics Roman Catholics are no more caught in this than other Christians. I cite the example only because the Pastoral Letters of the bishops would make possible a discussion of both issues, but that discussion is almost everywhere resisted.

37. This contradiction especially sends mixed messages to children and young people. As the commoditization of all of life is encouraged, it is difficult then to imagine that sexuality is an exception to the general rule of promiscuity on which our consumer society is dependent.

1. The Enlightenment offer of unfettered freedom without accountability is an unreachable mirage, an illusion never available to us.

2. The neat and conventional antithesis between law and grace is a distortion of faith, because there are no unconditional or conditional relationships in the gospel, but only relationships of fidelity that prize both freedom and accountability, the two always intertwined and to be negotiated.

3. Baptism is induction into the revolution of the coming rule of God. Like every revolution, this one has demanding disciplines that distinguish its adherents from all others.

4. Baptism is an acknowledgement of our true desire, our eagerness to be with, commune with, delight in, and delight through glad obedience to this life-giving holy Other.

5. It is precisely in our most primary zones of sexuality and economics, that the demands and desires of this alternative life are most demanding and most satisfying. Those demands and desires consist not in the voiced demands of conventional morality nor in the self-indulgence that is an alternative to the flat demand, but in the struggle for the interface of freedom and faithfulness which requires endless interpretive work and reflection.

6. Rejection of disciplines of the revolution and the distortion of our true desire may take place either through flat, one-dimensional traditionalism or through self-indulgence. Such rejection and distortion constitute a betrayal of baptism, and an attempt to live at least some of our life outside this coming rule, and according to the rules of the kingdom of death.

7. Willingness to join the revolution or to practice this core desire can never be coerced. Such engagement is possible only by those who perceive their true identity in this coming rule. And then the disciplines and desire are winsome, joyous, and life-giving, not at all burdensome.

Him, Him, Him

In the core Mosaic proclamation of Deut 6:5–6, immediately following the summons that Israel should listen (*shema'*), Israel is told:

> You shall love Yahweh your God
>> with all your heart,
>>> and with all your soul,
>>>> and with all your might.
>
> Keep these words that I am commanding you today in your heart.

Moses nicely juxtaposes *love* and *keep commandments*, because doing the will of the beloved is the way we enact love. Moreover, commandments are to be kept "in your heart," that is, they are not extrinsic, imposed, or coerced, but inhaled and embraced as one's own true will and intention.

This core summons is fleshed out in Deut 13:4:

> Yahweh your God you shall follow,
>> him alone you shall fear,
> his commandment you shall keep,
>> his voice you shall hear (*shema'*),
> him you shall serve,
>> to him you shall hold fast.

In this series of imperative verbs of obedience, two matters may be noticed. First, in Hebrew in this English translation, the word order is inverted to give emphasis to the object of the verbs, "him . . . him . . . him . . . him." It is like a lover saying, "You, you, you." Martin Buber quotes such a prayer from Levi Yizchak, rabbi of Berditchov:

> Where I wander—You!
> Where I ponder—You!
> Only You, You again, always You!
> You! You! You!

When I am gladdened—You!

When I am saddened—You!

Only You, You again, always You!

You! You! You!³⁸

Second, the last phrase that the NRSV renders "hold fast" (*dbk*) is elsewhere "cling," as in Gen 2:24. It is a term of deep loyalty and devotion, a kind of personal, passionate attachment that far outruns any external, extrinsic rule. Moses envisions a relation of affectionate trust.

Finally, in Mark 10:17–22, Jesus does "pastoral care" for a person who seeks "meaning" in his life. Jew that he is, Jesus responds to the man by asserting that the assurance he is seeking is found in full obedience to Israel's core commandments. Jesus assumes the man already knows the commandments. Beyond the commands, Jesus moves to "second-level" obedience: "Go, sell what you own, and give the money to the poor Come, follow me." It is as though the commandments are elemental, "first-level" access to the revolution, but serious pastoral care moves to a more radical reorientation of life.

We observe three items in this narrative. First, Jesus does not impose the commandments upon the man. The commands are not Jesus' idea. They are already there and already known at the beginning of the exchange. They are a premise of the conversation to which Jesus can make appeal. Jesus credits the man with knowing them, so that there is not a cubit of coercion in the response Jesus makes to the man's serious inquiry. Nonetheless, the response of Jesus is indeed a serious one. A good future is to be shaped by what is known of who God is, and what God desires.

Second, Jesus loved the man (v. 21). Good pastoral care depends upon such a positive disposition toward the subject. Such love, however, does not lead to the romantic easiness of unconditional acceptance. It leads rather to truth-telling which concerns obedience. Nothing imposed, nothing harsh, nothing quarrelsome,

---

38. Buber, *Tales of the Hasidim: The Early Masters*, 212.

only uncompromising truth-telling about the shape of well-being, spoken in love.

And third, Jesus' love, plus the assumption of the commandments, leads to a startling new demand, a demand too heavy for the questioner. The man decided not to join the revolution and decided to hold to his other "desire" of great possessions.

There is no anger or scolding in this meeting. We are not told that Jesus loved him any the less for his decision. But Jesus' love toward him, like that of Moses, is obedience-shaped. Jesus was clearly not much committed to "membership growth" in his little flock under revolutionary discipline. The difficulty of course is that truth-telling about well-being in a promiscuous society declares our common desires to be deathly. Obedience thus takes the form of alternative desire. When the holy one is supremely desired, is the "joy of loving hearts," obedience becomes joy, and duty becomes delight. Such a claim is difficult in the midst of misperceived Enlightenment freedom and in distorted "free grace." But that in itself is no reason to doubt its life-giving truth.

Israel knew that obedience is the path to genuine life. The commands are a mode of God's grace:

> The law of Yahweh is perfect,
>> reviving the soul;
> the decrees of Yahweh are sure,
>> making wise the simple;
> the precepts of Yahweh are right,
>> rejoicing the heart;
> the commandment of Yahweh is clear,
>> enlightening the eyes;
> the fear of Yahweh is pure,
>> enduring forever;
> the ordinances of Yahweh are true
>> and righteous altogether.

More to be desired are they than gold,[39]
    even much fine gold;
sweeter also than honey,
    and drippings of the honeycomb. (Ps 19:7–10)

39. It is worth noticing that the term "desired" is *hmd,* the same word that is rendered "covet" in the commandment Israel properly covets, that is, desires the commandments, the same desiring done by the couple in the garden in Genesis. Israel is supposed to "desire." It matters decisively what Israel desires.

2

I Will Do It . . . But You Go

MOSES WAS DOING AN ordinary thing, living an ordinary life, herding ordinary sheep. And then—in the midst of his life—the extraordinary, the miraculous exploded (Exod 3:1–12).[1] It moved in against him, addressed him, summoned him, and his life was changed irreversibly. The Bible does not quite know how to talk about that intervention (as we do not know how to speak about it), because the experience falls outside our usual way of talking. So the Bible speaks about a "bush burning," and an odd voice.

The real issue for Moses, however, is not the bush. What happened is that God came to confront Moses, and to give him a large purpose for his life that refused everything conventional. The reason we hold on to this old story and continue to ponder it is that we are people who either have had this extraordinary reversal of our life by God, so that nothing is ever the same again, or we wait for and yearn for such a moment that will break our life open. We hold this story because we know there is more to our life than the ordinariness of life without the holiness of God.

1. For further discussion of Exodus 3, see Childs, *Exodus*, 47–89; Fretheim, *Exodus*, 51–66; von Rad, *Moses*; Coats, *Moses*.

God of the Ancestral Stories

The first thing that happens in this moment of extraordinary miracle is that God speaks. God announces for God's own self a very specific identity. This is no generic God. It is rather the specific God of the book of Genesis: "I am the God of your fathers, the God of Abraham, the God of Isaac, the God of Jacob" (v. 6). And the statement might have added, "I am the God of Sarah, the God of Rebekah, the God of Rachel." I am the God of the old ancestral stories; the one who came upon hopeless old people and gave the children and new life; the one who came among wandering sojourners and promised them land; the one who came where life was all closed down and promised them a future they could not imagine or invent for themselves.

The first part of this story of Moses and the bush is a life-changing assertion: there are promises from God writ large in the faith of Israel and Judah, the church, and the life of the world. This story (and we) believe that God has indeed made promises and God will keep promises that run beyond all our controlled definitions of reality.

The alternative to promise is despair, which is what you get without the intrusion of this God. There are two kinds of people who despair. There are those who have nothing and who conclude they will never get anything. There are those, by contrast, who have everything, and who want to keep it just the way it is. Both those who have nothing and those who have everything find promises impossible. Nonetheless, God's promises are rude and relentless. These promises do not honor our despair or our complacency. We are the people who believe that God's future will cause a newness in the world, in which our old tired patterns of displacement and fear and hate cannot persist. In this "bush-narrative" God has come to enlist people into these promises for the future of Israel and the future of the world.

God's Intention for the Present

But second, God speaks to Moses not only about the old promises and future expectations. God comes to speak also about God's immediate intention for the present tense:

> I have seen the misery of my people . . . I have heard their
> cry on account of their taskmasters. I know their sufferings,
> and I have come down to deliver them from the hand of the
> Egyptians, and to bring them to a good land . . . I have seen
> how the Egyptians oppress them. (Exod 3:7–9)

The God of the Bible takes notice of social suffering in which some are oppressed and others are oppressors, in which some are exploited and others are comfortable because of the exploitation. God notices and God cares, and God acts decisively, because God will not put up with these kinds of dysfunctional social arrangements.

There is presently a great quarrel in the U.S. church about the nature of biblical faith and the God of the Bible. Is this faith only about matters religious and pious and private . . . or is it also about the great public questions of justice and equity in relation to economic and political reality? The argument is made differently here and there in the Bible. In this text we are discussing, we are at the core claim of biblical faith. The God of the Bible is profoundly and perennially preoccupied with the kind of human suffering that comes when one brother or sister is able to establish economic and political leverage over another brother or sister. Because God is who God is, there must be liberation and transformation, and the reestablishment of equity, a community in which all attend to all.

In the epistle lesson of Romans 8, which the lectionary juxtaposes with Exodus 3, Paul, good Jew that he is, knows about God's resolve for liberation.[2] In an astonishing way, Paul extends that resolve for liberation so that it concerns not just slaves and peasants and nomads, but the whole of creation. Imagine the whole of creation destined for an Exodus liberation!

---

2. On Romans 8, see the detailed discussions in Jewett, *Romans*, 474–554; and Käsemann, *Romans*, 212–52.

> The creation waits with eager longing for the revealing of
> the children of God . . . and the creation itself will be set
> free from its bondage to decay and will obtain the freedom
> of the glory of the children of God. (Rom 8:19–21)

What a mouth full . . . which Paul wrote long before our environment concerns. As Israel is enslaved to Pharaoh, so the creation is
enslaved to fear and anger and alienation, cursed under the distortion of the human community. And so creation cannot be fully
liberated until true "children of God" appear, who can care for the
earth differently. So says Paul, God wills the liberation of the world
in order that the creation can be its fruitful, productive, harmoni-
ous true self.

Notice that in these two speeches on *the promises of Genesis* (Exod 3:6) and on the *resolve of liberation* (vv. 7–9), Moses is
inducted by God into some of the largest and most definitional
themes of biblical faith. We Christians are people who attest to the
promises of God, believing that the promises of God are at work in
the world, unsettling every status quo, and making the world new.
We Christians are people who celebrate God's resolve for liberation, in society and in creation, knowing that God wants us all to
be liberated selves in a liberated creation. We affirm that the large
forces of God's promise and God's resolve are at work, even though
the world does not notice, and even though we ourselves do not
always resonate with that work.

God's Work and Human Work

After the promises to Moses and the announcement of liberation
to Moses, however, something very strange happens in the text of
Exodus 3. In vv. 7–9, God has uttered a lot of first person pronouns
in which God takes initiative for what must come next:

I have observed the misery of my people . . .

   I have heard their cry . . .

      I know their sufferings . . .

         I have come down to deliver them . . . and to bring them up . . .

        I have also seen how the Egyptians oppress them.

God is deeply, directly, and personally involved in this crisis in Egypt and intends to do something about it. Upon hearing this speech of God, Moses must have thought, "This is indeed some impressive God—God is going to do all this, even though I do not know how it will all happen."

And then there is an odd, surprising turn in the rhetoric. The same God who has been uttering all these "I" statements now says to Moses: "So come, I will send you to Pharaoh to bring my people Israel out of Egypt" (v. 10). "I will, I will, I will . . . so come, *you* go." What a turn around. The trick is that all of these glorious things God has resolved to do are now abruptly assigned to Moses as human work. It is, moreover, dangerous human work. You be the liberator! You go to Pharaoh! You go to the big house and confront the entrenched, oppressive powers. You care enough to make the case for this people in bondage. What had been "I, I, I," is now suddenly "You, you, you."

What happens in one quick rhetorical flourish is that *God's wondrous resolves* are transposed into *dangerous human work*. That is how it is lots of times in the Bible. God does God's work, to be sure; but the story of the Bible is the story of enlisting and recruiting human agents to do the things that God has promised. As you know, the book of Exodus is the tale of Moses' courageous life lived in defiance of Pharaoh for the sake of God's liberating resolve. Indeed, the resolve of God would not amount to much without the risky courage of Moses.

Now I assume you are like Moses and like me . . . ordinary life, ordinary work, ordinary sheep to tend. Nonetheless, it does happen that the power of God explodes in our midst, and we get pushed out beyond our conventional horizon. It is of course possible to go on, as though God's intrusion has not happened. Most of us, moreover, are timid and not inclined to crawl out very far on a limb. But it does happen, here and there, to people like us. And where it happens, the story of the church moves to its next scene, for the story of this people is the story of folk who have agreed to do the work which is God's own work of promise and liberation.

I imagine, moreover, that the reason we need to think about this story of the bush and its unsettling invitation is that we are in a society in deep crisis. It is clear that most of our old patterns of life together are not working. I suggest that this is indeed a time when the church may gather its faith together in order to think and pray and act differently. We are the people who believe that God's old promises for well-being and justice still persist in the world. We are the people who believe that God's resolve for liberation in the world and of the world is a resolve of urgency that still pertains to the abused. And we are the ones who know that the promissory, liberating work of God devolves upon folk who do God's work in the world.

So Moses had has ordinariness broken. He had to rethink about the faith of his people. Moses discovered that his life was saturated with the reality of God. And some God this is! The psalm assigned to the Exodus lectionary reading speaks of the God of the bush in this lyrical way:[3]

> . . . who forgives all our iniquity,
> . . . who heals all your diseases,
> . . . who redeems your life from the pit,
> . . . who crowns you with steadfast love and mercy,
> . . . who satisfies you with good as long as you live,
> so that your youth is renewed like the eagle's,
> . . . who works vindication and justice for all who are oppressed.
>
> (Ps 103:3–6)

And Moses wondered: What could be different about the purpose of my life because of the reality of this God?

---

3. On Psalm 103, see further, Brueggemann, *Message of the Psalms*, 160–61; Kraus, *Psalms 61–150*, 288–94.

3

Mission as Hope in Action

THE TOPIC "MISSION AS Hope in Action" brings into suggestive configuration three crucial accents that may preoccupy us in Lent.

Hope is the beginning point. It is *a human enterprise* rooted in God's faithful promises, acting constructively toward a future intended but not in hand, acting in resistance against a settled present for the sake of the future to be given by God.

Mission is an undertaking wherein *faithful human response* converges with God's resolve for the future of the world. It is an enterprise convinced that something is to be done, to be enacted, not yet in hand but undertaken in the sureness that God will see the future through.[1]

1. The transposition of *the mission of God* into *the mission of God's people,* a dominant theme in what follows, will alert us to the issue of "synergism," the risky thought that the obedient people of God may "help" God. I suspect that our conventional ways of putting this issue are at fault, for the reality of "synergism" is inescapable in the theme, even if the objectional label may be avoided. Consideration might especially be given to the strange poetic parallelism of Judg 5:11:

. . . there they repeat the triumphs of Yahweh,
the triumphs of his peasantry in Israel.

The poem is not worried, in the parallelism, to claim the victory for both

Action is *the risky human engagement* in a concrete, bodily way—powered by hope, shaped by missional imagination—in order to make a difference in the world, to reconfigure the interplay between God's intention and the reality of the world.

All three terms are oddly evangelical—rooted in the gospel; such an enterprise makes no sense in the conventional world that eschews hope, reduces mission to vested interest, and seeks only actions without life-or-death risk. Thus a bid for missional, hopeful action is always a summons to move outside whatever conventional world we inhabit.

A Call to a New Vocation

As the font of this odd configuration that is gospel-rooted, we may consider the strange case of Moses in Exodus 3. Israel's storytellers signal at the outset that coming to this gospel-shaped version of reality is no ordinary thing, precisely because it is rooted in the elusive, enigmatic account of the burning bush (Exod 3:1–6). That is, it is rooted beyond our explanatory capacity, shrouded in hiddenness with a staggering power to disrupt and to compel the subject (Moses) into a wholly new vocation, a calling of *active, missional hope.*

From the bush comes the utterance of the holy, hidden One (Exod 3:7–10). This utterance is completely unexpected by Moses, ungrounded in any of his categories of expectation, a vocation-creating *novum* in which Yahweh makes promises that set the world in a new direction. The promises are grand and evocative of Moses' hope. From now on Moses will be a hoper, completely convinced of a coming future for his slave community that falls outside the known world of Egyptian exploitation. The promise is a serious first-person, self-announcing declaration by Yahweh:

> I have observed the misery of my people,
> I have heard their cry,

Yahweh and the peasants. Our theme invites such thinking that can perhaps only be done in caring poetic parallelism.

>I know their sufferings,
>
>I have come down to deliver-to bring to a good land.

The cry of oppression has caught the attention of the Holy One who is now moved to take new action (see Exod 2:23–25). God will do all this. It is sure, not in doubt. This is God's own mission, to create a community of well-being from among the oppressed, outside imperial abusiveness. That is where the narrative is headed; Yahweh takes the initiative by this promise for the future of Israel, the future of Egypt, and the future of the world.

But then, in v. 10, the oracle of promise turns unexpectedly to Moses as an imperative: "I will send you." Until v. 10, the mission was Yahweh's; Moses could hear of Yahweh's intention with elation. In that verse, however, the mission of Yahweh becomes the mission of Moses. Moses is to run the risks that will guarantee a new social possibility in the world. It is Moses who must directly confront the powers of the empire with the alterative of emancipation. The Exodus, intended by Yahweh, is to be wrought by human daring and courage. The mission of God—now the mission of Moses—calls for concrete action in the empire.

It does not surprise us that Moses firmly resists this awesome assignment, offering in quick succession five objections (Exod 3:11—4:17).[2] The objections are attempts to evade active responsibility, to resist missional responsibility, to leave things with "master and slaves" as they are, undisturbed by Yahweh's missional initiative.

But of course this mission-initiating God will not let the mission-resisting Moses off the hook. The five resistances are readily answered by Yahweh's five responses, and the responses of Yahweh are in the end more important than the objections. Yahweh's assurance is essentially a reiteration of the promises of 3:7–9:

>"I will bring you out" (v. 17);
>
>"You shall not go empty-handed" (v. 21).

---

2. See Brueggemann, "The Book of Exodus," 713–17.

In the end, Yahweh will take full responsibility: "Who gives speech to mortals? Who makes them mute or deaf, seeing or blind? Is it not I, Yahweh?" (4:11).

Moses' resistances rooted in fear are vetoed by Yahweh; he is sent on his dangerous mission before the court of Pharaoh. For all the robust rhetoric of Yahweh, however, he has nothing to go on except this sovereign insistence of fidelity that requires his courageous activity. And of course, it is this mandate, rooted in holy power, that brings him to pharaoh and sets in motion the defining emancipation in the story of the world.[3]

Cancelation and Reparation

For our purposes and for the ministry of Lent, however, the Mosaic embrace of "Mission as Hope in Action" is too exotic, too daring, and too spectacular for almost any of us, even if he is the paradigmatic case of our faith. Fortunately, Moses himself provides a more mundane and concrete model for the matter, albeit still risky. In Exod 3:21, as noted, Moses assured the Israelites that "you will not go empty-handed" (see 3:22; 11:2; 12:36); Moses authorizes the frontal transfer of wealth from the imperial "haves" to the escaping slave "have-nots." The catch-phrase "empty-handed," as David Daube has observed, turns up in Moses' pivotal teaching in Deut 15:13 concerning the "year of release" (Deut 15:1–18).[4] This instruction, unlike the narrative account of Exodus 3, contains nothing as elusive and enigmatic as a burning bush and nothing as risky as direct confrontation with Pharaoh. Rather it proposes a hands-on, completely doable economic act that is designed to enhance the neighborhood.[5] The "year of release" provides a policy and procedure for the limitation on debts and requires that "haves" recognize "have-nots" as neighbors who are to be cared for and

---

3. On the generative power of the Exodus narrative for a powerful continuing trajectory of revolution, see Walzer, *Exodus and Revolution*.

4. Daube, *The Exodus Pattern in the Bible*, 55–61.

5. On this text, see the important study of Hamilton, *Social Justice and Deuteronomy*.

protected, so that they can participate viably and with dignity in the economic interaction of the community. Moses affirms both that this act of debt cancellation is urgent because there are always poor people in debt (v. 11), and that if this year of release is done diligently and generously, there need be no poor people (v. 4). Moses understands that it is the deep and defining practice of long-term debt that eventually disables community. The "empty handed" teaching in v. 13 provides that the poor shall not only have debts cancelled, because left empty-handed they will soon cause their debt to reappear, so that positive *reparations* are required beyond debt cancellation for the sake of the community.

Clearly the move from *burning bush* to *year of release* is to descend, as it were, from heaven to earth, from exotic religion to mundane economics. Our topic, moreover, suggests high-grade religious commitment and accomplishment, rather like old-fashioned notions of "winning the world" for the Gospel. But biblical faith and biblical ethics are more characteristically earth-bound than that. The leap from burning bush to year of release is a characteristic move of covenantal faith, a move from *gift of God* to *love of neighbor.* While we notice the profound contrast between the two assertions of Exodus 3 and Deuteronomy 15, we might for our purposes more profitably notice the commonality in these two acts that are in resistance to being "empty-handed."[6] Indeed, the action authorized in the statute of Deuteronomy 15 is a repeatable Exodus enactment, whereby the ancient narrative miracle is presented as a necessary habit of the ongoing community. The year of release brings the indebted neighbor "out of the house of bondage" even as the slaves in Egypt were enslaved as debt-slaves (see Exod 20:2). Thus the Exodus itself is an enactment of the year of release. As the statute of Deuteronomy 15 does not want the poor in the community to be empty-handed, so the narrative of Exodus 3 provides that the slaves departing Egypt will not be empty-handed.[7]

---

6. In both Exod 3:21 and Deut 15:13, the term is "empty" (*rîq*). The same usage, as Daube has noted, is surely intentional.

7. See also Exod 11:2; 12:35–36.

The commonality between the two, narrative and statute, pertains to all three elements of our theme.

Hope: The Exodus is rooted in God's own hope for a new people in a new land. The year of release is rooted in God's assurance, everywhere expressed in Deuteronomy, that the land of Canaan can and will be reorganized in covenantal, neighborly ways. Specifically, Deuteronomy 15:18 concludes with a promise, "Your God will bless you" when you act in neighborly ways. The anticipated blessing that grows out of neighborliness is clearly an act of hope.

Mission: It is God's mission to emancipate the slaves from Egypt and to bring them to a new land, a mission that is assigned to Moses on behalf of Yahweh. It is God's mission, in the vision of Deuteronomy, to reorder the community of neighborliness, a goal that becomes the missional obligation of every Israelite in covenant toward neighbor. The practice of a generous economy is indeed a missional undertaking, not religiously exotic, but stark and daily.

Action: The mission grounded in hope requires concrete, bodily, daring action. Moses must run the risk of appearing insistently and defiantly before the court of pharaoh. The mandate for action in the instruction of Moses is not as dramatic as the Exodus. It nonetheless requires concrete, bodily, risky action, namely, the cancellation of debts that gives the enhancement of the neighbor priority over personal profitability. The risk dimension of this missional action is evident and readily recognized when this biblical teaching is commonly regarded as "unreal" or at least only applicable to a small, agrarian economy, both attempts at evasion.

The linkage of *hope, mission and action,* so the Bible teaches, is grounded in God's own holy resolve. In the Lenten season, however, it is important to recognize that the practice of this revolutionary, emancipatory faith takes the form of steady, daily, bodily, intentional neighbor acts.[8] The "sacrificial" dimension of faith,

8. These steady, daily, bodily, intentional neighbor acts might properly be termed "habits" in the sense that Robert Bellah et. al., *Habits of the Heart: Individualism and Commitment in American Life*, have made central to the current discussion. These sorts of habits are more readily understood and appreciated when we consider the "habits" of consumerism that television

35

about which we characteristically speak much in Lent, concerns the ceding of priority over to the neighbor, for what this hope-based mission will not tolerate is leaving a neighbor empty-handed. The refusal of empty-handedness for the neighbor of course invites endless parlor games about "the public sector" and "the private sector." All of that, however, is secondary to the mandate and the vision that is consistent in our faith from the miracle narrative to the covenantal statute. What counts, rather than economic theory or ideology, is the *God who hopes* and the *neighbor who needs.* The mission, humanly speaking, is to enact a workable, transformative *connection* between *God's hope* and *neighbor need.*

The Hope of God in the Life of Jesus

Now of course, a focus on Moses, the Exodus, and the instruction of Deuteronomy does not first of all leap to mind in the Lenten season of the Church. I suggest that it would be a useful connection to make in the church to see that the hard tale of the Passion Narrative of Jesus from Friday to Sunday, is a closely retold tale of Israel's move through wilderness to the new land.[9] The instructions of Deuteronomy, moreover, are paralleled in the demands of discipleship on the lips of Jesus en route to death and then new life. The discipleship to which Jesus summons his people is not to be found in exotic religious acts, but in the slow, daily work of bringing the neighborhood under the rule of the one whose kingdom is "at hand." The parallel is indeed worth the effort, because in both cases of ancient Israel and early Church, as in our own case as church, the story concerns an *alternative vision of the life of the world under the rule of the slave-freeing, wound-healing, covenant-making God.* This alternative vision is rooted in the will and purpose of God; but it is practiced concretely in risky, bodily acts by the people of this God.

---

ads seek to engender. Indeed, these *neighbor habits* are an alternative to and an act of resistance against the dominant *habits of consumerism* in our society.

9. Wright, *Jesus and the Victory of God,* has nicely shown the important ways in which Jesus reenacts the story of ancient Israel.

The hope of God in the life of Jesus is given in those spectacular moments of enunciation, birth, baptism, and transfiguration that lie beyond the critical reach of the Jesus Seminar.[10] Those events with their enormous generative power can no more be decoded than the burning bush can be extinguished by Moses. In these events, the God of all hope gives Jesus the authority to anticipate and to create a future that is not available apart from the coming rule of Jesus.

The mission of God—namely the restoration of viable life in creation—is of course *the mission of Jesus*. Jesus' ministry makes clear that the rescue and rehabilitation of creation is not done in one huge salvific act; it is rather done leper-by-leper, widow-by-widow, and neighbor-by-neighbor:

> Go and tell John what you have seen and heard: the blind receive their sight, the lame walk, the lepers are cleansed, the deaf hear, the dead are raised, the poor have good news brought to them. And blessed is anyone who takes no offense at me. (Luke 7:22–23)

Jesus' life consists in *teaching* and *action* that makes the mission of God effective and the future of God visible.[11] These enactments are not done by some safe, dismembered, heavenly being, but only by costly, bodily contact with real people in the real world. Thus in the healing of the hemorrhaging woman, Jesus perceived that "power had gone forth from him" in a *body-to-body transaction* concerning this fleshly work of God (Mark 5:30). The claim made for Jesus by the early church is very large, and indeed becomes even larger when the tale is recast by the church into creedal abstract language. But the tale told that sustains creedal claims is a

---

10. These several spectacular episodes that shape the gospel narrative are not unlike the narrative of the burning bush in marking the narrative by epiphanies that defy our explanations. They provide the driving energy, in both cases, for the concrete narratives that follow.

11. It surely is the case that teaching is an action that, when done effectively, has transformative potential. See Green, *Voices: The Educational Formation of Conscience*.

tale of neighborliness, the vision of heaven brought down to earth in concrete cases.

The Church Replicating Jesus' Transformative Power

Of course the servant is not above the master (Matt 10:24). What Jesus enacts the church after him must repeatedly enact. Not for nothing is the story of the early church presented as *Acts,* "deeds," embodied, risky actions implementing the mission under the aegis of God's promise. The encounter of Acts 3:1–10 exhibits the early church replicating the transformative power of the Jesus in the world toward the neighbor. Peter and John are clearly "hopers," hoping that what they know in Easter and Pentecost is the world's future, perhaps cosmically but certainly for this lone beggar in front of the temple. Their mission, as the mission of Jesus, is to restore creation in this creature to fullness of being. The mission characteristically is beggar-by-beggar, lame man by lame man, made to walk and leap and praise God (Acts 3:9). They did this! It is their *act*! It is an act of the apostles, of the apostolic church. It is *an act of hope* committed in the wake of Jesus who himself enacted the neighborly alternative of God for the world.

The mission is not dangerous until it gets to specific acts. And then, we are told, only a chapter later:

> the priests, the captain of the temple, and the Sadducees came to them, much annoyed, because they were teaching the people and proclaiming that in Jesus there is the resurrection of the dead. So they arrested them and put them in custody until the next day, for it was already evening. (Acts 4:11–13)

Think of it; the response is "annoyed," "arrested," "in custody"! All because they had produced restoration, a surge of life that will challenge and override the debilitating status quo.[12] The apostles

12. Parallel to the way in which the apostles could override the status quo, Moses' action in the Exodus is the same sort of act, albeit more spectacular and generative for what follows after him. The essential work of the act in the two cases is closely paralleled. The way in which healing characteristically

dare proclaim . . . and they dare enact![13] The outcome is this man "walking and leaping and praising God," calling into question the shut-down of a world without hope.[14] The authorities seek to keep the lid on hope with all of the official, legitimated gravitas of despair. They will, however, never stop "the force," no more than could pharaoh.

The Church Contradicts the World

Lent is a demanding time for pastors. It is demanding, of course, because of time and work pressures. More than that, it is demanding because in its narrative of emancipation and wilderness en route to newness, *the church contradicts the world*:

- It asserts *hope,* because God has made promises;

- It asserts *mission,* because God has assigned the vision to human agents;

- It *acts* to rehabilitate the neighbor, precisely when the fashion of this age is to reduce, deprivilege, and make the neighbor invisible.

Lent is for contradictions that we ourselves can scarcely tolerate, for it renders the conventional unbearable and the inscrutable

---

evokes resistance in the gospel narrative is worth noting, no doubt arising because the adversaries of Jesus, like Pharaoh, had "hard hearts" (see Mark 2:6–7; 3:5). "Proclamation, like teaching, is an act. As every totalitarian regime knows, utterance is the most dangerous threat to the maintenance of a monopoly of power. Both teaching and proclamation are acts of defiance against the silence upon which oppressive monopoly depends.

13. Proclamation, like teaching, is an act. As every totalitarian regime knows, utterance is the most dangerous threat to the maintenance of a monopoly of power. Both teaching and proclamation are acts of defiance against the silence upon which oppressive monopoly depends.

14. The "new man" made possible in this narrative by the dangerous subversion of the apostles is deeply reminiscent of the dancing and singing of Miriam and the women in Exod 15:20–21. These eruptions of joyous freedom are an enactment of new possibility that, both in this narrative and in the Exodus narrative, the status quo intended to prohibit.

palpable and nearly commonplace. Such a bodily enactment, body-to-body, contradicts all the *consumerism* that substitutes "virtual" for the bodily and all the *new ageism* that seeks to escape the bodily into "higher matters." We should expect resistance to Lent, as Moses resisted. Indeed, we ourselves resist, too good to be true, too hard to be embraced, too bodily to be religious. The God of the self-assertive "I" transposes all of God's own purposes into a missional "you." We will resist the mandate for a while, but probably not finally. Before the "I" of Yahweh, our resistance is at best penultimate action.

4

The Proclamation of Resurrection in the Old Testament

EASTER IS THE EXTREME case of God's sovereign action. The resurrection of Jesus must not be trivialized around a biological question of resuscitation of a dead body, nor around questions of curiosity about immortality or life after death. That Jesus is risen is not a statement about heaven, but about the transformation of earth.

New Governance over Death

The theological assertion the church has found in the resurrection of Jesus is that here God has powerfully asserted a new governance over the toughest region of creation, namely death. Read through a theological prism, the course of world history is the arena through which God gains authority over creation, some parts of which are readily accessible and compliant to God's rule, and other parts of which are haughty, resistant, recalcitrant, and not easily accessible.[1] Where Yahweh's power is not effective, the

1. Barth has most powerfully articulated this region not yet responsive

power of evil-chaos-injustice-oppression-despair-death (all of which are synonyms) has its way. But when God's rule is asserted, that part of creation is transformed into good (Gen 1:31), order (Isa 45:18–19), justice (Ps 99:4), freedom (Lev 25:42), hope (Lam 3:21–24), life (Ps 23:2). The theological claim is that a new rule has been established, that Yahweh governs now as Yahweh did not before. God's sovereign domain is not once-for-all given, but it is in process and God is through history gaining dominance even in regions not immediately attainable. The actual experience of that new governance is the prospect, gift, and possibility of human life in the world as God has willed it. The news that is to be asserted in evangelical preaching is that the world situation, that is, the condition of creation, has been transformed by the effective power of God that is the only power for life. Theologically, the resurrection of Jesus is the extreme case against the last recalcitrant region (1 Cor 15:26), but God's governance of death is not different from what God has been dealing with in all seasons of God's life with the world.

Schmid has helpfully asserted that justification by grace, creation *ex nihilo,* and resurrection of the dead are synonymous theological assertions of the powerful action of the creator governing the world and bringing the world to its full life (cf. Rom 4:17).[2] That three-fold parallelism opens enormous possibilities for preaching. Such an understanding of the resurrection requires at the beginning a criticism of our cultural habit of reading the resurrection as a magical individualistic act of resuscitation, and instead seeing that event (as the Bible surely does), as a show of God's massive power. Or as Schmid says, it is the establishment of God's magisterium (*Herrschaft*) over the whole world. Preaching from this faith then engages with the other would-be governances of the world that are in this event nullified.

---

to God, which he characterizes as "this stubborn element and alien factor" (*Church Dogmatics,* III/3, 289–95).

2. Schmid, "Rechtfertigung als Schöpfungsgeschehen," 403.

Creation out of Chaos

We may identify three paradigmatic assertions in the Old Testament of extreme cases of God's sovereign action against recalcitrant creation. The preaching task is to communicate the ways in which these same theological issues are still the decisive ones for us. Such preaching of course must challenge the benign trivialization through which modernity perceives life, to see (a) that *sovereignty* is still the decisive question of human existence, (b) that *conflict* is still alive between rivals, and (c) that *transformation* happens when this sovereign displaces other claimants to power and authority.

The first paradigmatic assertion is that God has wrought creation out of chaos (Gen 1:2) and that that change has been done by Yahweh's powerful sovereign word (Ps 33:6–17). The world pre-Yahweh, pre-creation, pre-sovereign speech is dark, formless, void, without power, without shape, without meaning, without a significance (Gen 1:2). Yahweh's sovereign speech calls that chaos to shape up. Creation responds promptly, willingly, gladly. Indeed the world is celebrative and delighted when Yahweh finally takes charge, permitting the world to be what it must be and what the world has hoped to be (cf. Ps 96:11–12; 98:7–8). Now creation can get on with its business of fruitfulness, abundance, and prosperity (cf. Hos 2:21–23; Ezek 34:25–27).

The claim the Bible makes about creation must not be presented as an explanation of the origin of the world. Rather that claim, as asserted in Genesis 1 and Deutero-Isaiah, is a liturgical assertion that has experiential immediacy for concrete situations of chaos. Critical consensus is that the text of Genesis 1 reflects the sixth century exile, which seemed like a shapeless, hopeless context. The priestly liturgy of Genesis 1 wants to assert that this exilic context is one in which Yahweh rules by a powerful decree, "Let there be light." Therefore, even that context is not without power, hope and possibility.

Every pastor deals with folk for whom life is experienced as chaos, in terms of personal concerns and family problems. And public affairs in our time are often discerned to be chaotic. There seems to be no reliable power to count on, no constant shape, and no overriding meaning. Life is indeed chaotic. Preaching in such a context requires the assertion that what appears to be chaotic is precisely an arena in which God's powerful purpose for life is being worked out. If one reads from the "good" of Gen 1:31 to the "good" of Gen 50:20,[3] what the powers of darkness intend for evil is a way in which God intends and implements good. That is what creation faith asserts. This assertion has immediacy and pertinence for people in the midst of chaos.

Exodus from Oppression

The second paradigmatic event is the Exodus. Here the problem is not chaos but oppression. Nobody accused the Egyptian government of being chaotic (just as nobody accuses the South African government of fomenting disorder). If anything, the Egyptian empire was too tightly ordered, so tightly ordered that persons were discounted in the flow of imperial power, in the rush of imperial programs, and in the harshness of brick quotas. The liturgical enterprise of Exodus 1–15 is at pains to characterize fully the harshness and hopelessness of the situation (Exodus 1 and 5). The middle narrative of the plagues in Exodus 5–10 dramatically presents the conflict of Pharaoh versus Yahweh, of life versus death, of oppression versus liberation.[4] The conflict is long and tense. In its dramatic portrayal, that conflicted question could finally go either way, toward oppression or liberation, toward death or life.

But of course the liturgical drama does not leave the issue unresolved. The liturgical outcome in the narrative of Exodus 14 and in the lyrical poem of Exodus 15 asserts and celebrates that Yahweh, the God of justice and liberation, has won. There may

---

3. On this envelope of "good," see Dahlberg, "On Recognizing the Unity of Genesis."

4. On the revolutionary impetus of this narrative, see Walzer, *Exodus and Revolution*.

be dancing, singing, and living, because the power for justice and liberation will not be co-opted by the forces of injustice.

The preaching task at Easter is to show how this paradigmatic event (happily celebrated in Passover at Easter time) is pertinent to and being acted out in our own lives. The issues of justice and liberation are so incredibly visible and urgent among us. One senses the awesome power of justice and liberation on the move in Tunisia, Egypt, Bahrain, Yemen, and Syria. Those events need theological, liturgical articulation. But this paradigm draws closer to home. People in rat-race jobs know about relentless brick quotas. Persons in distorted family situations know about oppression, injustice, and the hopelessness of it all. The evangelical news is that every such situation stands under judgment, but also under transformative possibility, because even there Yahweh's new governance can matter in decisive ways. Those who groan under the burden (Exod 2:23–25) may dance with Miriam in new life (Exod 15:21).[5] Preaching is the dramatic invitation to embrace that new reality.

Homecoming from Exile

The third paradigmatic event is the homecoming from Babylonian exile in the sixth century. That this is portrayed as a resurrection event is precisely stated in Ezek 37:1–14, so that this connection is explicit. But it is in the poetry of Isaiah 40–55 that the transformative gospel of the end of exile is asserted. The poetry of Isaiah 40–55 utilizes both paradigms already suggested, that of creation out of chaos, and liberation out of slavery.[6] Indeed in this poetry we are offered a powerful convergence of most of Israel's theological traditions, all of which bespeak the gospel. The word "gospel" here for the first time is used with theological intentionality by

5. On the song of Miriam and the related corpus, see O'Day, "Singing Woman's Song: A Hermeneutic of Liberation."

6. On the use of the tradition in Deutero-Isaiah, see Anderson, "Exodus Typology in Second Isaiah"; and Anderson, "Exodus and Covenant in Second Isaiah and Prophetic Tradition."

Deutero-Isaiah (Isa 40:9; 52:7). The news is that Yahweh's sovereign power permits the alienated, displaced ones to go home.

The "world of death" is here a situation in which the power of Babylonian governance and Babylonian gods seem absolute and beyond challenge. The sense of displacement, despair and alienation is articulated with powerful pathos in the book of Lamentations and in such psalms as 137. "Exile" means to be in a place where one's dreams are mocked, one's convictions devalued, and one must live without a sense of belonging.

The news rendered by this poetry is that Yahweh, who is like a man of war (cf. Exod 15:1; Isa 40:10) and like a gentle nursemaid (Isa 40:11), has moved powerfully against Babylon, and has reestablished the rule of covenant which seemed defeated by the realities of the exile (Isa 42:6; 49:8; 54:10; 55:3). That new assertion of governance happens through the historical agent, Cyrus. It leads to the dethronement of Babylonian gods (Isaiah 46), the delegitimation of Babylonian power (Isaiah 47), the lyrical offer of a new song (Isa 42:10), and finally to homecoming (Isa 43:3–7). The displaced Jews are going home. There they will be safe and honored, no longer mocked or devalued. The situation is decisively changed when Yahweh's rule is asserted.

The sense of displacement and the yearning for homecoming is not remote from people in our context. The displacement happens because of a variety of cultural changes of revolutionary proportion that mean we are no longer "at home." Berger suggests that modernity makes us "homeless,"[7] without a center for belonging, so that we are endlessly alienated, exhausted, and fatigued. The news is that the power of alienation is robbed of its authority (cf. Eph 2:14).

Faithful people are invited to home-building in the midst of the alienation.[8] There can be home-building in the midst of alienation because Yahweh rules over this seeming exile which is no longer exile. The very place of alienation when ruled by God

---

7. Berger, Berger, and Kellner, *The Homeless Mind*.

8. See Teilhard de Chardin, *Building the Earth*.

becomes our home. This is what it means to find "grace in the wilderness" (Jer 31:2).

These three paradigms amount to the assertion of life in the face of death: ordered creation in place of chaos, liberation and justice instead of oppression, homecoming in the place of exile. The power of the Bible that permits powerful preaching is that its central conviction lives very close to human experience, because every person knows about chaos, oppression, and exile. Every person waits for order, liberation and homecoming. Easter is the occasion when the Church celebrates "the extreme case," but that case of Jesus occurs in the midst of other cases that are not dissimilar.

Modes of Articulation

Creation, Exodus, Homecoming are the substantive material of resurrection faith. We may also give brief attention to the modes of assertion of this transformative governance of God. It will not do to assert this transformation in language that is flat and descriptive, for that is inadequate and not fully convincing.[9] The modes of articulation are important for Easter preaching.

1. The transformative victory of God's governance consists first of all in *doxologies of sovereignty* which are liturgical songs flung in the face of ostensible reality. One cannot argue with the deathly reality of the world on its own terms, but must change the terms of the debate. For example, one cannot bring life from quoting statistics about the relative weaponry strength of the U.S., Russia, and China, but one must speak in a different mode so that life can be experienced differently. Easter faith is first of all sung faith and Easter preaching must be very close to lyrical. The preacher then need not (and indeed must not) engage with the "reasonableness" of modernity, but stands at a different place and speaks from a different conviction.

Thus the great assertions of the Bible are doxologies that include the great enthronement Psalms (Psalms 96–99), the lyrical

9. On the cruciality of language for the church's reception of this faith, see Wilder, *Theopoetic*.

liturgy of Genesis 1, the celebration of the Song of the Sea (Exod 15:1–18), and the celebration of Cyrus (Isa 45:1–7). It is singing that is thrown in the face of would-be rivals. The lyric, therefore, turns out to be polemical. The doxology not only sings Yahweh to the throne, but it sings chaos-Pharaoh-Babylon out of power. Such singing mocks and finally dismisses all the phoney claims to power (cf. 1 Cor 15:55).

2. A second mode of the transformative Easter power of Yahweh is presented in *narratives of inversion.* These are stories in which the plot of the narrative is a transformation of circumstance or persons, so that what was trouble at the beginning is resolution at the end.[10] Perhaps the most obvious and normative narrative is that of the Exodus (Exodus 14) which forms a counterpart to the doxological song in chapter 15. At the beginning of the narrative Israel must still face the oppressive power of Pharaoh (14:5–9). But at the end of the account (14:30–31), Egypt is dead and Israel lives in faith and freedom. The narrative mode is crucial because only the story form can present the strange, unexpected inversion that is logically inexplicable. Easter faith does not explain, but only testifies and narrates.[11]

This thrust of narrative can be played out in various forms. It is the structure of many of Jesus' "miracles" which are also Easter narratives. Thus the themes include hungry/fed, blind/sight, lost/found, dead/alive. Moreover the compelling power of the narrative mode is that the hearer in subsequent time not only listens to an old account of inversion, but participates in the present enactment of the story. The power of such preaching is to include the listening congregation in the happening of the story as it is told and heard one more time with astonishment that outruns explanation. All

---

10. On this structure of narrative, see the study of Culley in *Studies in the Structure of Hebrew Narrative* and the numerous examples he cites. This structure of inversion is what Via means by the "comic" structure of the gospel (see *Kerygma and Comedy in the New Testament*).

11. This peculiar mode of articulation is related to what Richard R. Niebuhr means by "historical reason" (see *Resurrection and Historical Reason*). One can argue that the resurrection narratives are the quintessential historical narratives.

of these narratives (including the resurrection stories of the New Testament) are not told simply as historical record, but that the listening community may appropriate the inversion as also operative in its own life. Thus at Passover time, the Exodus story is retold each year as a present enactment of liberation. The Easter preacher is not to tell an old story as a recollection, but to let it be a present dramatic reality in the life of the congregation. That is how "the old, old story" becomes "the new, new song."

3. Derivative from these two modes of *doxologies of sovereignty* and *narratives of inversion* we may suggest a third mode in which to speak about Easter. Easter faith is not immediately pertinent if it stays only with cosmic or grand public events. Israel also found it possible to identify the same assertion of God's life-giving governances in personal accounts of transformation in songs of thanksgiving, in *personal witnesses of amazed gratitude*. These songs are the voice of individual persons who are not grand public figures but who in quite personal, daily ways have found that the move from chaos to order, from oppression to freedom, from alienation to at-homeness, from death to life has happened in their own experience.[12] Psalm 30 is a marvelous example of this personal appropriation and practice of the public claim of Easter faith:

> I cried to thee for help,
>> and thou hast healed me.
> O Lord, thou hast brought up my soul from Sheol,
>> restored me to life from among those gone down to the pit . . .[13]
> Thou hast turned for me my mourning into dancing;
> Thou hast loosed my sackcloth
>> and girded me with gladness . . . (Ps 30:2–3, 11)

---

12. Albertz, *Persönliche Frömmigkeit und offizielle Religion*, has fully characterized this more personal, intimate faith that lived alongside the religion of the great cult. See also Albertz, *A History of Israelite Religion*, 2 vols., 1:25–39, 94–103, 186–95; 2:399–410, 507–22.

13. On the metaphor of the "pit" in the Psalms, see Brueggemann, *Praying the Psalms*, 32–42.

No explanation is given. This is only narrative testimony of a quite personal kind, the kind anyone might make when the gift of life wells up in our midst. But such occasions do happen. And when they happen, they must be told (cf. Ps 22:22). The power of God toward life is known in concrete, specific ways. Yet when persons are ready to speak about personal interventions from God, characteristically they use the language and speech forms of the great public paradigm of the Exodus. While our tendency is to fashion language out of private experience, Biblical faith begins with public speech that is then appropriate for personal experiences. Verbs like "heal" and "brought up" are language that in Israel derives from the Exodus memory (cf. Exod 15:26). This aspect of testimony permits the preacher to identify the turn toward life that happens in all kinds of ways for those who have faith to see and tongues to tell. It is from people who know the Exodus story is still operative in their lives (Deut 26:5-9) that the Bible has come. And from such people comes the current testimony that keeps faith credible, even midst modernity.

Advent of the Promised Kingdom

I conclude with four comments:

1. The challenge of Easter preaching is a substantive theological one. The preacher and the congregation must be clear that God's governance is being asserted. Where that rule is asserted, new life is given in transformative ways. The resurrection is a claim that counters the hopeless, reduced life around us where God's rule is neither expected, discerned, nor celebrated. A substantive decision is required of us, for modernity has eroded even our readiness to hold to this miraculous scandal. Unless we are clear about this claim, there can be no empowering preaching of this act of God.

2. When that substantive decision is made (and always made again), the problem is to find a universe of discourse that does not concede too much. How shall we speak of this reality that our world cannot tolerate? The ways in which the Bible speaks are alien to our flattened modes of technical reason and to our culturally

distorted notions of how life is given. The modes of doxologies of sovereignty, narratives of inversion, and personal witnesses of amazed gratitude are Israel's preferred ways. None of these modes squares with technical epistemology that is incapable of doxology, which does not believe in inversions, and which refuses to be amazed. But these matters of life and faith cannot be expressed in the tongues of modernity, for it is this very epistemology that has consigned us to death and despair.

3. All three modes that speak this strange speech are powerfully subversive. Easter faith not only testifies to God's new sovereignty. Conversely it also dethrones, delegitimates, and dismisses old sovereignties that are now discredited and defeated. Easter means the dismissal of Pharaoh, Caesar, and all imperial power. Easter means the dismantling of all the pathologies by which we order personal, family, and public life. This preaching will soon bring preacher and congregation into conflict with entrenched pseudo-authority. Thus Elijah's raising of the boy (1 Kgs 17:8–16) is a prelude to confrontation with King Ahab (1 Kgs 18:17–19; 21:20–24) who does not want the power of God unleashed in his controlled, drought-stricken world.

4. Easter occasions are not isolated events that happen in a vacuum. Easter occasions are beginnings of new processes that endure and have futures. They are occasions when power is unleashed that continues to permit and summon us to life. Thus in Genesis 1, the creation event not only permitted the world, but gave humanity an ongoing vocation (v. 28). Thus in Exodus 1–15, the liberation from slavery not only let Israel be, but urged Israel to Sinai to receive the Torah and embrace a new obedience. So also the resurrection of Jesus has permitted and summoned the church to a new mission. New life is never just an isolated momentary event. New life becomes a force and energy that stays active against the resilient power of death.

The theme of Easter preaching has peculiar urgency in our context. I believe that Easter preaching about the transformative power for life given in the sovereignty of God is now a matter of critical importance among us. Our culture in its dominant values has embraced the power of death in so many destructive ways. This strong power of death will shrivel our humanness as it has already begun to do. I propose that it is precisely the tongues of serious evangelical preachers (by which I mean voices of the gospel) which can counter this sickness to death (Rom 10:14–17). Easter preaching is not some magical, spiritual consolation, but it is engagement with the rulers of this age. Everything depends on this sovereignty being brought to new speech (Isa 52:7).

In his answer to John's need for Christological clarity, Jesus gives a series of Easter evidences:

> The blind receive their sight,
>> the lame walk,
>>> lepers are cleansed,
>>>> the deaf hear,
>>>>> the dead are raised up,
>>>>>> the poor have good news preached to them.
>
> (Luke 7:22)

These are all of a piece. They concern human reality. They are an affront to our closed worlds (cf. Luke 7:23). But nevertheless they are true and waiting to be discerned, spoken, embraced and practiced. Such preaching leads to dangerous discipleship that enacts the power of transformation. Amos Wilder comments on the power of resurrection: "It was not a question of Jesus' deliverance from death as a separate miracle but of the advent of the promised kingdom of God."[14] The kingdom for which we pray in the Lord's Prayer can become visible in Easter preaching which asserts that the prayer has been answered. The kingdom is on the move, and is coming soon!

14. Wilder, *Theopoetics*, 95.

5

The Commandments and Liberated, Liberating Bonding

THE PEOPLE OF ISRAEL had just departed from the Egyptian empire. They were clear on only two things. First, they would no longer submit to the brick quotas of the empire. Second, Yahweh the Holy God was the great new fact and force in their life. Indeed, it was precisely Yahweh who had uttered the liberating decree, "Let my people go" (Exod 5:1; 7:16; 8:1, 20; 9:1, 13; 10:3). And they had gone! Pharaoh had not wanted them to go, because they were cheap labor. But they had gone. Yahweh was so powerful that Pharaoh could not stop the power of Yahweh for liberation. Now they are free.

Embrace of a New Bonding

In saying, "Let my people go," Yahweh had also said, "that they may serve me" (Exod 5:1; 7:16; 8:1, 20; 9:1, 13; 10:3). The Exodus was not an offer of unbridled, unqualified, unfocused freedom that had no projection into the future. The Exodus was to embrace a new bondage, that is, a new bonding (cf. Lev 25:42).[1] The oppressive bonds of Egypt are broken. Now the liberating, covenantal bond of Yahweh is offered. Israel makes its way to Mt. Sinai for the new bonding, to be linked in a covenant with Yahweh that displaces its submission to Pharaoh. Everything for Israel is at stake in this exchange of bondage for bonding.

They arrived at Mt. Sinai. It was an awesome meeting, rooted in the awe of God's holiness. The meeting with Yahweh is enveloped in the terror, splendor, danger, and inscrutability of God's theophany (Exod 19:16–25).[2] God comes powerfully into the midst of Israel. God's massive presence intrudes. God's overriding purpose pervades. Israel is caught up in a purpose more powerful than it can comprehend, in a presence more sovereign than it could imagine. The *awe of theophany* moves to the *offer of covenant*. The holy God of liberation commits God's own life to solidarity with Israel. This God is not ashamed from now on to be known as the God of Israel, to be with, care for, and preside over the life of Israel (Heb 11:16). Yahweh's intention for Israel is not simply a moment of liberating, but an on-going life together in covenant.

But on the way from the awe of theophany to the offer of covenant, there are terms, conditions, stipulations. The centrality of law in Israel means that Yahweh has a determined moral intention for this relation. The God who goes with Israel is not merely an available patron, but a sovereign who will out-govern the empire. The Ten Commandments are the decree of the inscrutable God for the shape of the new bonded relationship. These commands as decrees are to be taken as non-negotiable terms for this alternative to the empire. They are policies that require interpretation, but they set the character and shape for new life.[3] They specify who

1. On the implications of the new bonding at Sinai, see Buber, *Prophetic Faith*, chap. 5; and more fully, Buber, *Kingship of God*, especially chaps. 7 and 8.

2. On this theophany, see Terrien, *Elusive Presence: Toward a New Biblical Theology*, chap. 3.

3. Mendenhall first saw that the Decalogue constitutes "policy from which other law is derived" (*Law and Covenant in Israel and the Ancient Near East*, especially 3–6).

God will be in Israel, and they make concrete the institutional life of this odd community whose destiny is in contrast to the empire.

The preacher's task is to set the commandments, the burden of obedience, in the context of the liberating memory. More than that, the preacher's task is to set the listening community in the context of the Exodus story, so that it becomes our story. We are the ones who have been offered a liberation from the empire. We are the ones invited to a new bonding in covenant. We are the ones who watch in awe for the inscrutable presence and power of Yahweh. We are the ones who have been graced with the terms on which new life is possible. That is why the commandments begin, "I am Yahweh who brought you out of the house of bondage." What an opportunity for the preacher, to invite the congregation to begin acting outside the loyalties and possibilities, policies and prospects of the empire!

On this beginning point for obedience, church people need help,

in seeing that *deliverance* from imperial power which dehumanizes and crushes *is now available* for us.[4]
in knowing that the *alternative* to the empire and its killing brick quotas is not unqualified, autonomous freedom, but brings *a new summons to obedience*,[5]
in trusting that the terms of *covenant law are an offer of bonding freedom* which is the only lasting freedom that can be.[6]

The crucial relation between Exodus and Sinai, between liberation and bonding, is at the center of our preaching task. This

4. I have explored the grip the empire has on our imagination under the rubric of "royal consciousness" in Brueggemann, *Prophetic Imagination*, chap. 2.

5. On the powerful temptation to autonomy and unmitigated freedom as an ideology, see Bellah et al., *Habits of the Heart*.

6. On the yearning in our society for more serious bonding, see Yankelovitch, *New Rules: Searching for Self-Fulfillment in a World Turned Upside Down*. Remarkably, even Masters and Johnson came to see that real "pleasure" requires some bonding (*The Pleasure Bond: A New Look at Sexuality and Commitment*).

preaching now occurs in the American church between two mistaken temptations. On the one hand, there is the mistaken notion that we are rightfully and dutifully children of the empire, so that our proper destiny is to conform politically, submit economically, obey morally whatever power is in charge.[7] The Exodus narrative refutes such a conformist posture, because we are destined for the liberation given from God from every such tyranny, political, intellectual, theological (cf. Gal 5:1).[8] On the other hand, there is the mistaken notion that having been made free, we are free to do whatever we want and be whomever we choose. The Sinai narrative refutes such a notion by asserting that the God who liberates is also the one who sets the terms for a human future. Preaching on these matters must attend to both mistaken notions, and on the central claim that true liberation is in trust and obedience to the God of the Exodus who binds us in a new bonding—outside the deathly reach of the empire. That is why the Lord of Sinai begins in self-identification with the Exodus: "I am the God who freed you from slavery."

An Alternative to Conformity and Autonomy

The purpose of the Decalogue is to confirm in social, sustained, institutionalized, community form what has been begun in the events of Exodus.[9] The shape of the Decalogue sets the perimeters for a new life that is not oppressively conformist and that is not unrealistically autonomous. The Christian preacher with these texts may help the congregation to think through an evangelical alternative to oppressive conformity and destructive autonomy, an alternative that is experienced as faithful covenanting.

7. See Soelle, *Beyond Mere Obedience*.

8. Walzer has exposited the revolutionary impetus contained in the Exodus narrative (*Exodus and Revolution*).

9. Harrelson has well explored the potential in the Decalogue for matters of social policy and the institutional shaping of public life (*Ten Commandments and Human Rights*).

It is well known that the Decalogue easily divides into two "tablets," first concerning relation to God, and second, concerning relation to neighbor. To sustain the new freedom initiated in the Exodus, these two relationships must be maintained faithfully, knowingly, and with discipline.[10] If either relation is distorted, the covenant vision of Sinai is put at risk.

New life in covenant requires a faithful, undistorted relationship with God. The clue to this proper relation is to remember that the God of the covenant is the God of the Exodus. The God who there acted to liberate is the God who wills continued liberation in the community. The God who is to be honored and obeyed in covenant is none other than the one who had compassion for and solidarity with the slaves, and who had authority and power over the rulers of the empire. The covenant community willed by this God is a community that continues to practice compassion and solidarity, and which maintains vigilant criticism against every totalitarian agent and ambition.

Israel's life as a covenant community depends on a clear vision and a sharp memory of who God is. To forget this radical character of God is to engage in idolatry, to imagine a God who is not so free, dangerous, powerful, or subversive as is the God of the Exodus. Israel is tempted to tone down Yahweh's compassion for and solidarity with the powerless, to make God a bit more compatible to social "realism." Or Israel seeks to tone down the abrasive power of Yahweh against oppressive powers for the sake of some modest, provisional accommodation to the rulers of this age.

But the liberating, sovereign presence» and purpose of Yahweh asserted in the commandments is not negotiable and must not be toned down. Idolatry consists in harnessing God for our purposes, regarding Yahweh as a reliable ally in our interests, so that God finally becomes useful to us.[11] That usefulness is a temp-

---

10. Hall has suggested a third decisive relation with the non-human world (*Imaging God: Dominion as Stewardship*). While he is surely correct, that relation lies outside the explicit structure of the Decalogue.

11. On the theme of "usefulness" as a distortion of God, see Brueggemann, *Hopeful Imagination*, chap. 4.

tation of all zealous religion, conservative or liberal. The same usefulness is practiced by political ideology, for example, in Israel's old
royal-temple establishment, or in some contemporary claims that
God is "with us" and endorses our way.

The second (Exod 20:4–6) and third (Exod 20:7) commandments exposit this claim of the sovereign liberating God who will
be obeyed but not used, who will initiate new life for us, but will
not conform to our arrangements of life. To shun "graven images"
means that God's power for life must not be captured in ideology or program or institution.[12] To avoid "using the name" means
that God's power must not be domesticated by us and for us. Thus,
positively these commandments assert God's faithful power that
takes initiative for new life. Critically the commandments function
as a warning against our temptation to "enlist God" in our best ef-
forts to have life on our own terms. The recovery of the powerful
freedom and free power of God is an urgent and critical task of the
preacher in our cultural setting that on the right harnesses God to
our social inclinations, and on the left trivializes God away from
God's proper role in our life.

*New life in covenant requires a faithful honoring and taking se-
riously covenant neighbors and the proper use of covenant property.*
New life entails sorting out who are persons to be honored and
cared for, and what is property to be properly used. The "second
tablet" insists that neither persons nor property are to be abused,
that is, enlisted for other than their true purpose. Commandments
five through ten are assertions about the kind of caring neighborliness that is indispensible for a community of covenant that will
not degenerate into a society of abuse, disrespect, oppression, and
finally brutality. The commandments are a line drawn against brutality. These commandments insist that persons do not *earn* stand-
ing in this community, but they are *entitled* to an honorable place
simply because they belong in the community. Again the Exodus
memory is decisive, for it insists that the first liberated slaves received a new option for life from Yahweh, not because of merit,

12. On the social power of contemporary idolatry, see Richard, ed., *Idols of
Death and the God of Life: A Theology.*

but because Yahweh had freely entitled them to it, according to Yahweh's sovereign, compassionate decree. That same sovereign, compassionate decree of entitlement is and must be operative in the community evoked by Yahweh. This linkage of neighborliness as social policy and the Exodus is made explicit by Moses: "Love the sojourner therefore, for you were sojourners in Egypt" (Deut 10:19).

The entitlement of communal dignity is extended to old people who have lost their usefulness to society: "Honor your father and your mother" (Exod 20:12).[13] The entitlement extends to the valuing of all members of the community, all of whom are to be given life and let live: "Do not kill" (Exod 20:13). The entitlement extends to familial relationships, in which binding loyalties are to be honored and taken seriously: "Do not commit adultery" (Exod 20:14). The entitlement extends particularly to the poor and defenseless who are not to be confiscated into debt slavery: "You shall not steal" (Exod 20:15).[14] The entitlement extends to the right of all for justice, so that the courts are to stand as a defense and protection against distorted public power and public administration: "Do not bear false witness" (Exod 20:16). Finally and decisively, old land boundaries of inalienable family land are to be honored and not perverted by sharp, commercial business or legal practice: "Do not covet" (Exod 20:17).[15] This climactic commandment is to protect the weak in their small landholdings against the

13. On the ethics of the elderly in the Bible, see Harris, *Biblical Perspectives on Aging: God and the Elderly*.

14. Here I am accepting the persuasive hypothesis of Alt, "Das Verbot des Diebstahls im Dekalog." Alt argues on the basis of the texts like Deut 24:7 that the command originally had a direct object, "Do not steal a man," and prohibited kidnapping in which the object was sold into slavery. More generally on the commandment, see Gnuse, who relates the commandment more directly to economic policy and practice (*You Shall Not Steal: Community and Property in the Biblical Tradition*).

15. On the commandment, see Chaney, "Thou Shalt Not Covet Your Neighbor's House."

great power of government or those connected with the levers of government.[16]

The neighbor commandments derive from the radical claim of God's holiness in the first three commandments. God's holiness must not be domesticated. Alternatively, the dignity and value of the neighbor must not be violated.

While we may think of other areas of community life that should be brought under the claims of covenant, commandments five through ten are an astonishingly comprehensive statement concerning dimensions of life to which the covenantal will of the liberating God is pertinent. The promise of the new liberating bonding is forfeited when persons are reduced to commodities, when the fragile social fabric of community is reduced to a set of technical transactions, when entitlements as free gifts from God are reduced to merit as a basis of worth or productivity.[17] It is clear that the commandments envision a community that continues to be at work in liberating its members from all practices that cheapen, enslave, or brutalize.

In viewing the two tablets about a faithful, undistorted relation with God, and a serious concern for covenant neighbor and covenant property, we may observe the relation of the first and tenth commandments. The first (Exod 20:3) concerns the truth of God concerning God's holiness, compassion, and freedom. The tenth commandment (Exod 20:17) concerns right land relations in which the weak do not have their proper life-space taken from them. In considering the first and last commandments together, it is evident that Israel understood the close relation between the holiness of God and the humanity of the community. It is for that reason that the two "great commandments" are held together (Matt 22:34–40; cf. 1 John 4:20–21). Or negatively Israel understood that idolatry always leads to exploitative land policy (coveting). The

16. Chaney takes Mic 2:1–5 as an important interpretive comment on the tenth commandment. He follows the suggestive proposal of Alt, "Micah 2:1–5." More generally on Micah as a critic of rapacious social policy, see Wolff, "Micah the Moreshite—The Prophet and His Background."

17. Heschel has most eloquently articulated this crisis in our understanding of humanness in modernity (*Who Is Man?*).

preaching task is to make clear and understandable an inextricable relation between a distinct discernment of heaven (the character of God) and a distinct discernment of earth (the organization of social power in the community). Distortion in either of these leads to a dual distortion that ends either in death in a disordered community, or oppression in a tyrannical community that has returned to the dehumanizing ways of Pharaoh.

The Sabbath as Center and Focus

It may be observed that in the above analysis of the two tablets, I have not commented on the fourth commandment concerning sabbath (Exod 20:8–11). That is because this commandment concerns both tablets and cannot be placed simply with either.[18] Indeed, the sabbath commandment functions as the center and interpretive focus for the entire Decalogue, and therefore as the center of Israel's ethical reflection. The commandment looks back to the *rest of God.* It dares to affirm that Yahweh (unlike imperial gods) is so well-established, so surely in charge, so greatly respected by creation, so gladly obeyed by all creatures, that God's governance is not one of anxiety or franticness. The world is confidently, serenely ordered as God's good creation. That affirmation can lead to a "basic trust" among us about our place in the world.[19]

The commandment also looks forward to the practice of the human community. It asserts that responsive to God's well-believed governance, the human process in the world is not, and must not become, an endless rat race of achievement, productivity, and self-sufficiency. Rather the goal and crown of life in the community of covenant is the freedom, space, and delight of sabbath

---

18. On the cruciality of the sabbath commandment in the Decalogue, I am indebted to the discerning analysis of Miller, "The Human Sabbath: A Study in Deuteronomic Theology."

19. I am of course appealing to the poignant phrase of Erik Erikson, but I intend it not simply in a psychological mode but in a more inclusive way as "at-homeness" in the world.

rest.[20] In keeping sabbath rest, the human community replicates and participates in the tranquility God has ordained into the structure of creation. Sabbath as that "sacrament of basic trust" is sociologically radical, for it invites all members of the community to be in well-being and peace, without reference to power or position. Indeed, the commandment envisions an act of radical egalitarianism modeling new social relations for in that day, "Your servant will be *as you*" that is, entitled to equal rest.[21] One can hear in this commandment echoes of the powerful egalitarianism of the Exodus. In the empire there is no day when slave is like master, but in covenantal sabbath practice there is such a day for "as you," when all social class distinctions and differentiations of power are dramatically criticized, jeopardized, and overcome. In this commandment, Israel acknowledges *the precious rule of God* that is not harsh or anxious, and *the precious possibility of human community* that, in imitation of God's generous governance, oppresses none. Taking this command as the center of the Decalogue, we suggest that the entire Decalogue proposes an ordering of heaven and earth that is radically different. It is not modeled after conventional modes of power, but after the astonishing transformation of the Exodus. The commandments envision a community so ordered that such liberating work goes on as the normal way of ethics.[22]

The Interpretive Work

I suspect that the most difficult and most important task for the preacher with the commandments is to handle the absoluteness of the commandments, while at the same time doing the required

20. Heschel who has so wisely exposited our human crisis has also well and eloquently under stood the alternative carried in the Sabbath, *The Sabbath: Its Meaning for Modern Man*. For Heschel the sabbath is the source of any alternative to our rampant profanation of human life.

21. See Wolff, *Anthropology of the Old Testament*, 139–40.

22. Childs has presented a suggestive exposition of the Decalogue, especially stressing its theonomous claim (*Old Testament Theology in a Canonical Context*, chap. 7).

interpretive work necessary to faithfulness.[23] It is clear that for biblical faith, the Ten Commandments are absolute and non-negotiable, taken as God's sure decree. It is, however, equally clear in the Bible itself that Israel and the church maintained and practiced amazing *interpretive openness* in order to keep the commandments pertinent to the ongoing ethical burdens of the community in various changing circumstances.

Both points are important. The absoluteness and the non-negotiability must be stressed against a kind of moral softness or indifference that dissolves or trivializes the ethical claims of biblical faith. The non-negotiability must be insisted upon, even when it strikes some as authoritarian. Conversely, the need for interpretive openness must be stressed against every legalism and moralism that imagines all the questions are settled, and so makes the character of command cold and unresponsive to the realities of life. That interpretive openness must be insisted upon, even when it strikes some as relativizing the claims of the covenant.

Non-negotiability and *interpretive openness* must be held together in order to avoid both imperial absoluteness and destructive autonomy. I will take the fourth commandment on Sabbath to illustrate this point. It is clear that:

- The Bible takes this command with abiding seriousness, and

- The Bible continues to struggle with and reinterpret the claim and intention of the command.

As the Bible itself is engaged in an open interpretive process, so the preacher may seek to engage the congregation in an interpretive process to ask how the liberating will of the covenant God is to be enacted among us.

It is clear that the sabbath commandment is part of an ongoing interpretive tradition in which we can participate. The commandment is neither dismissed as unimportant, nor is it treated as flatly and absolutely obvious. It is and must be interpreted. Among

---

23. On the need for interpretation to keep a timeless document timely, see Tracy, *Analogical Imagination*, chaps. 3 and 4, esp. 102.

the critical points in that on-going work of interpretation are the following:

1. The version of the commandment in Deut 5:12–15 already departs from the Sinai version of Exod 20:8–11 by articulating a new motivation. Now the reason for the command is not that God rested on the seventh day of creation, but that Israel remembers the Exodus. Deuteronomy has handled the commandment in a sociologically more radical way by suggesting that sabbath is a sacramental reenactment of Exodus which delivers people from the imperial burden. This version focuses on community experience, not on the structure of creation.

2. Amos 8:4–8 indicates how the commandment is taken up into radical prophetic analysis. In this passage the sabbath command is said to function as a protection for the poor against sharp economic practice. Sabbath is a cessation from commerce so that the needy have a brief respite from relentless exploitation. The command becomes a ground for criticizing public practices in Israel that have become as abusive as any in ancient Egypt before that Exodus.[24]

3. In exilic and post-exilic thought, the sabbath became a crucial mark for the covenanted community, distinguishing it from those in the empire who had no memory of Exodus. Isaiah 56:2 identifies sabbath keeping as a characteristic mark for a blessed person, that is, one who enjoys the benefits of covenant. Then in vv. 3–7, sabbath is made the qualifying mark to admit foreigners and eunuchs to Israel's worship. That is, the command becomes the not very demanding entrance point through which unqualified people qualify for the covenant. The sabbath is a vehicle for countering extreme legalism that wanted to make requirements a good deal more stringent.[25]

24. See Lang, "The Social Organization of Peasant Poverty in Biblical Israel," esp. 58–59.

25. On the intention of Isaiah 56 in contrast to a more rigorous alternative, see Achtemeier, *Community and Message of Isaiah 56–66*, 32–37.

4. In his ministry Jesus violates the sabbath for the sake of humaneness. In Mark 3:1–5 he heals on the sabbath, and in 2:27–28 he gives his magisterial dictum that Sabbath exists for the sake of humanity. In Jesus' circumstance, the sabbath had become an oppressive practice of social control. Jesus' response is congruent with and derived from the notion of Exodus bonding, that is, acting against the commandment for the sake of liberation in the community. The commandment is valid, he seems to affirm, only insofar as it serves its intended witness to the Exodus as a mode for continuing life in covenant. Jesus' dangerous ministry is in rescuing people from many "houses of bondage" each of which has been constructed by commandments that have lost their Exodus orientation. Commandments which do not serve Exodus stand under harsh criticism.

The purpose of briefly presenting such a trajectory of interpretation for the commandment is to permit the congregation to see that while Israel takes the commandments with great seriousness, it practices interpretive openness so that the concern in each case is that the command be a vehicle for God's liberating bonding.

The contemporary church must criticize law and commandment that in fact enslave those who have been entitled. Thus the prohibition against killing, when read in the presence of the Exodus, sounds differently to oppressed peasants in Latin America. Or the command to honor father and mother is heard differently in a family where there is child abuse. Characteristically, serious evangelical faith understands the commandments as guides for God's liberating activity, and when they work against that liberating activity, they must be reconsidered, as Jesus does with the Sabbath commandment.

The purpose of such biblical preaching and teaching is not simply to exhibit interpretive diversity in the Bible (which in itself is worth doing). It is rather to summon the congregation to join this conversation about the commandments, to see what now this command may "mean" in order that liberated obedience may take place. In recent time we have had to work against excessive restrictiveness practiced in the name of sabbath in a puritanical society. But now we need to be asking what the sabbath command-ment means in a society that reduces humanness to technical transactions.[26] In such a society that reduces persons to commodi-ties, the acknowledgement of God's restfulness and the embrace of our own rest may make sabbath a crucial moral opportunity, and an important sacramental protest against the busy profanation of our common life.[27]

It is my suggestion that a similar and more detailed history of interpretation for each commandment could be identified in the Bible, and beyond the Bible in the history of the church. The purpose of such historical recovery for preaching is to nurture the congregation away from moralism to serious bonding, away from self-sufficiency to serious liberating responsibility.

An Invitation to Obedience

The Decalogue is an invitation to evangelical obedience, that is, obedience rooted in the gospel, the practice of which is genuine-ly good news. Such obedience is good news because it replicates God's own action in the world for us. It is good news because such obedience lets our actions come into agreement with our proper identity as slaves liberated by God, as children welcomed to the household of covenant. It is good news because such obedience makes a community of human bonding possible in a world dead set against serious human bonding.

26. Plaut writes: "I therefore view the sabbath as potentially an enormous relief from, and protest against, these basic causes of unrest. Once a week it provides us with an opportunity to address ourselves to the who-ness rather than the what-ness of life, to persons rather than to things, to Creation and our part in it, to society and its needs, to ourselves as individuals and yet as social beings" ("The Sabbath as Protest: Thoughts on Work and Leisure in the Automated Society," 177).

27. Tsevat says of the sabbath, "Every seventh day the Israelite renounces his autonomy and affirms God's dominion over him . . . Keeping the sabbath is acceptance of the sovereignty of God" ("The Basic Meaning of the Biblical Sabbath," 49–50).

The first task of the preacher, I suggest, is not explication of particular commandments. It is rather to show that the Bible believes that the liberating alternative set into motion in the Exodus continues to be a proposal for sustained, ordered social life. Because Yahweh is a different kind of sovereign, Israel is permitted to embrace a very different kind of obedience. This obedience is not the oppressive, despair-inducing obedience of the empire. Nor is it an obedience so rigid and narrow as that of some opponents of Jesus. It is an obedience rather, that is a genuine delight, because it makes humanness possible. No wonder Israel delights in the law (Ps 119:97). Such obedience is not conforming, but transformative (Rom 12:2). It requires our best intellectual effort because the intention of the commandments in every new situation requires fresh and careful, bold and daring articulation.

The preacher and the congregation can celebrate that we do not have to guess about God's main intention for us. That has been disclosed. But such faith still seeks understanding. Such commands still await specific implementation. Such liberated bonding still awaits the concreteness of covenant community toward brother and sister, toward land and property.

6

Truth-Telling as Subversive Obedience

THE NINTH COMMANDMENT—"YOU SHALL not bear false witness against your neighbor"—has not been an accent point in biblical ethics or an emphasis in Mosaic-covenantal faith. Moreover the commandment is easily reduced to a kind of banal moralism, as though "lying" is a bad thing and should be avoided, a notion that is as thin as one can make the commandment. We here reconsider this commandment both as an exploration in interpretive method, and to see how this commandment may be a primal carrier of a Mosaic-covenantal vision of reality that is oddly pertinent to our moment of social crisis.[1]

False Witness against Neighbor

It is important at the outset to recognize that the commandment, expressed in absolute terms, is part of the Decalogue given at "the holy mountain." As such it constitutes a part of the most elemental

---

1. For a parallel consideration of the fourth and tenth commandments, see Brueggemann, *Finally Comes the Poet*, 79–110; and Brueggemann, "The Commandments and Liberated, Liberating Bonding," in chapter 5 above.

insistence of the Sinai covenant.[2] More than that, it voices an important dimension of the Mosaic vision of social reality and social possibility.

The commandment brings into stark juxtaposition two terms that assure its covenantal intent: "neighbor—false." The prohibition is not simply against "false witnesses," but it is a false witness against *your neighbor*, that is, a fellow member of the covenant community. The horizon of the prohibition is the well-being of the neighbor and the enhancement of the neighborhood. More broadly, the prohibition concerning practices and conditions that make a neighborhood viable and genuinely human.

The antithetical term here is "false" (*šqr*). In the second version of the Decalogue, the term is *šw'* but the intention is not different (Deut 5:20). The term "false" concerns utterance that distorts or misrepresents or skews. Viable community, according to Mosaic vision, depends upon accurate, reliable utterance. The process of community is profoundly vulnerable to distorted speech that inevitably skews social relations and social structures.

The commandment, however, is even more particular. It alludes to the precise setting in which false utterance is possible, seductive, and dangerous. "You shall not answer with false testimony." The verb "answer" and the noun "witness" indicate that we are concerned with solemn utterance under oath in a judicial context. In short, the commandment seeks to assure a reliable, independent judiciary. The Ten Commandments, as a whole, seek to bring every facet of social life under the aegis of Yahweh and into the context of covenant. This ninth commandment concerns the court system, and insists that evidence given in court must be honest and reliable and uncontaminated by interest. It is astonishing that in its most elemental summary, Yahwistic ethics insists upon

---

2. The literature on the Decalogue is immense. In addition to the magisterial and normative interpretations of Luther and Calvin, see Harrelson, *Ten Commandments and Human Rights*; Childs, *Old Testament Theology in a Canonical Contexts*, 63–83; Lehmann, *The Decalogue and a Human Future*; Preuss, *Old Testament Theology*, 1:100–117; Miller, *The Ten Commandments*; and Brown, ed., *The Ten Commandments*.

a reliable, independent judiciary as one of the pillars of viable human life.[3]

It is clear that the notion of a court that gives reliable utterance is a continuing concern of the tradition of Moses. In Exod 18:13–23, offered as a Mosaic innovation, Moses is instructed to find reliable judicial officers: "You should also look for able men among all the people, men who fear God, are trustworthy, and hate dishonest gain" (v. 21).[4] And in speaking of judges subsequently,

> You must not distort justice; you must not show partiality; and you must not accept bribes, for a bribe blinds the eyes of the wise and subverts the cause of those who are in the right. Justice, and only justice, you shall pursue. (Deut 16:19–20)

The courts are seen to be crucial, because in social disputes which relate to political, economic matters, it is the capacity and responsibility of the court to *determine, limit, and shape reality.* And therefore if power and interest can intrude upon truth— by way of influence, manipulation, or bribe—then truth has no chance. It is reduced to power, and the powerless are then easily and predictably exploited.

Recent public events make altogether evident that a reliable, independent judiciary is indispensable to a viable society. In the U.S., it was the courts that were finally able to insist upon a constitutional vision of human and civil rights when all other aspects of the public process had failed. In old colonial powers and in the dictatorships of "banana republics," it is often only the judiciary that prevents legitimated exploitation and brutality. Indeed, even as I write this, it is a "truth commission" with something like quasi-judicial powers at work in South Africa which has a chance

---

3. A range of texts is related to this commandment and some perhaps derived from it: Exod 23:1, 6–8; Lev 19:11, 16–17; Deut 19:15ff.; Amos 2:7; 5:15; Mic 3:11; Pss 12:2; 27:2; 64:8; Prov 11:9–13.

4. There is a long-standing critical tradition that situates the judicial provisions of Exodus 18 in the context of Jehoshaphat's reform, on which see 2 Chr 19:4–11. While such a critical judgment may be made, the text as it stands makes a claim for Mosaic authorization.

to put to rest the long nightmare of brutality in that society. This commandment insists, in a direct and unadorned way, that "social truth" inheres in neighborly transactions and is not open to the easy impact of raw power that denies human reality. The commandment guarantees that *reality* is not an innocent product of *power*. The future of humanity is not open to endless "reconstruction" by those who have the capacity to do so, but must adhere to what is "on the ground."

The Prophetic Word

The commandment is likely articulated in a simple, face-to-face agrarian society. It is a simple requirement that neighbors not distort shared social reality. But as is characteristic in biblical traditions, this simple agrarian provision is transformed into a larger social concern by the imaginative power of the prophets. The requirement of truth-telling is matured by the prophets, first by enlarging its scope to include royal reality with its penchant for distorted public policy and second, by turning a "rule of evidence" into a Yahwistic claim. Examples of this larger maneuver include Nathan's word to David concerning the violation of Uriah (2 Sam 12:7–12) and Elijah's word against Jezebel who had manipulated truth by royal power (1 Kgs 21:19–24). In both cases, it is important that it is the issue of truth that is at stake in the prophetic confrontation. Both David and Jezebel have born false witness, David against Uriah, Jezebel against Naboth. Such distorting actions cannot stand, even if performed by the royal house.

In the prophetic period, powerful royal interests were skillful at the management of symbols and the control of information (disinformation) that scenarios of "virtual" reality could be constructed completely remote from lived reality. The tradition of Jeremiah is preoccupied with *falseness* whereby managed reality yields a phony sense of life and well-being.[5] The poet counters such control:

5. See Overholt, *The Threat of Falsehood.*

For from the least to the greatest of them,

everyone is greedy for unjust gain;

and from prophet to priest,

everyone deals falsely.

They have treated the wound of my people carelessly,

saying "Peace, peace,"

when there is no peace. (Jer 6:14; cf. 8:11)

Now the concern is not one citizen deceiving another, as it might have been in a neighborly, agrarian society. Now it is the great organs of news and information in society being managed to serve distorted public ends, calculated to deceive on a grand scale.

Working the same rhetoric, the prophet Ezekiel holds religious leadership peculiarly guilty for such programmatic distortion: "In truth they [the prophets] have misled my people, saying "peace" when there is no peace . . . When the people build a wall, their prophets smear whitewash on it" (Ezek 13:10).

These recognized voices of established reality deliberately misrepresent the true state of the economy and of foreign policy. Society has broken down and is not working, and they legitimate the dysfunction and give false assurance. The voices of accepted legitimacy present a fake reality, with failed fact disguised as workable fantasy. The prophetic traditions accepted as canonical are agreed that such fantasy will bring devastation upon a deceived community.[6]

We have here made a large leap from face-to-face neighborliness into the royal engine room of public distortion. With this leap, I may suggest three facets of "false witness" which invite to

---

6. The issue of false and true prophecy is an enormously vexed issue. While it may be claimed that there is nothing which formally distinguishes false and true prophets, it is clear that *in substance* ancient Israel, in its canonizing process, made important distinctions. For representative views of the issue, see Crenshaw, *Prophetic Conflict: Its Effect upon Israelite Religion*; and James A. Sanders, "Canonical Hermeneutics: True and False Prophecy." On the classic case of Jeremiah 27–28, see Mottu, "Jeremiah vs. Hananiah: Ideology and Truth in Old Testament Prophecy."

killing distortion. These distortions in our contemporary world echo those against whom the great prophets railed:

1. *Euphemism.* The use of euphemism consists in describing a reality by labeling it in terms that completely disguise and misrepresent. Long ago Isaiah had noted the capacity to deceive by giving things false names:

> Ah, you who call evil good
>> and good evil,
> who put darkness for light,
>> and light for darkness.
> who put bitter for sweet,
>> and sweet for bitter. (Isa 5:20)[7]

Those who control the media have vast opportunity for such sustained intentional distortion. Robert Lifton has chronicled the way in which the perpetration of the Jewish Shoah cast these deathly operations in "toxic euphemisms," so that the entire process of the death camps could be presented as a practice of medicine.[8]

In our own time, moreover, Noam Chomsky has characterized the ways in which the public apparatus is endlessly submissive to deliberate misnomer.[9] The deceiving work of euphemism—which is a public pattern of false witness against neighbor—is especially effective in two areas of our common life. First the entire military industry and the so-called defense program of the world's

---

7. The NRSV renders the first word "Ah." That innocuous translation is unfortunate, for the term bespeaks sadness at loss and death. The word indicates a sense of loss that is to come on those who practice deceiving euphemism. K. C. Hanson has argued that the Hebrew *hoy* should be translated "shame" and is the counterpart to *'ashre* "honorable"; see "'How Honorable!' 'How Shameful!'"

8. Lifton, *The Nazi Doctors: Medical Killing and the Psychology of Genocide*, 202 and passim.

9. Chomsky's argument in this regard is stated in many places. See for example, Chomsky, *Necessary Illusions: Thought Control in Democratic Societies*; Chomsky, *What Uncle Sam Really Wants*; and Chomsky, *The Washington Connection and Third World Fascism*. My own references are from a lecture he presented in June 1995.

last superpower are regularly disguised by euphemism, for the simple reason that a massive killing enterprise to protect inequity in the world dare not be called by its right name. This is evident in giving peaceable names for missiles capable of massive destruction. Second, in like manner, the rapacious free market economy delights in euphemism, in order to cover over the human pain and cost of extraordinary and unconscionable profits. Thus, as Chomsky notes, unemployment becomes "downsizing," "jobs" has now become a four letter word for "profit," and greed operates under the name of "opportunity."

2. The capacity for misrepresentation is especially poignant in television *advertising*,[10] which posits a never-never land born in the happy ways of the "product." In that land there is never pain, never hurt, never fear, never poverty, never any negation that is not overcome by "the product." One would not ever know from such ads that the gaps of rich and poor grow like a cancer in our society. The ads present a "virtual reality" enormously attractive but remote from where the world must be lived.

3. Closely related to advertising, is the incredible world of *propaganda*, which offers a vested interest as a totality of truth, which generates false certitudes and false loyalties that belie the reality of human life.[11]

The church in its accommodating timidity has characteristically wanted to keep the commandments of Sinai safely in modest zones of moralizing. It is unmistakable, however, that *euphemism, advertising, and propaganda* all serve to bear false witness against neighbor. And since dominant "word-making" and "world-making" are always in the hands of those who control technology, these pseudo-versions of reality are regularly the work of the strong

10. See especially Postman, *Amusing Ourselves to Death: Public Discourse in the Age of Show Business*; Postman, *Technopoly: The Surrender of Culture to Technology* (New York: Random House, 1993); and Postman, *How to Watch TV News* (New York: Viking Penguin, 1992).

11. The most important studies of the theme are by Ellul: *The Humiliation of the Word*; *Propaganda: The Formation of Men's Attitudes*; and *Technological Society*.

against the weak, the haves against the have-nots, the consequence is to make invisible and unavailable the truth of life in the world.

Truth-telling about God

The rhetoric of the courtroom operates where "truth" is unsettled, in dispute, and still to be determined. The ancient agrarian prohibition against false witness seeks to stop social distortions that make life brutal, exploitative, and unbearable. Against these propensities, the prophets urge that the deathly truth of the world must be told, a truth that characteristically lives and works at the expense of the weak.

Along with *the truth of the world* in its failure, however, this commandment concerns *telling the truth about God*. This may seem so obvious as not to warrant comment. Except that "God" is completely enmeshed in social-political-economic realities.[12] In order to maintain social advantage, it is often necessary to tell the truth about God in false ways, because the "really real," that is, the gospel truth about God is revolutionary, subversive, and disruptive.

In Deutero-Isaiah, we may see how this simple agrarian prohibition is now turned into a theological agenda whereby Yahweh is "the Neighbor" about whom the truth must be told. Israel must bear true witness to this Neighbor in the midst of exile. Some exiled Jews, apparently, had come to terms with Babylonian realities, accepted the legitimacy of Babylonian gods and engaged in Babylonian modes of life. That is, the claims of God had to be conformed—by false witnesses—to power realities. The prophet critiques "the witnesses" who submit to "idols" which can neither see nor hear nor do anything (Isa 44:9). Those false gods to whom false witness is given generate false lived reality.

12. Karl Marx has seen this with the greatest clarity and influence. Note his programmatic statement: The criticism of heaven is thus transformed into the criticism of earth, the criticism of religion into the criticism of law, and the criticism of theology into the criticism of politics.

The poet seeks to counter that entire cache of falseness by a summons to truth telling. Israel is to tell the truth about Yahweh, to be Yahweh's true witnesses:

> Do not fear, or be afraid;
>> have I not told you from of old and declared it?
>> *You are my witnesses!*
> Is there any god besides me?
>> There is no other rock; I know not one. (Isa 44:8)

In the preceding chapter, Yahweh asserts to the exiled Jews: "You are my witness" (43:10). And the testimony to be given concerns Yahweh's capacity to initiate an alternative in the world, to work a newness in society, to emancipate Israel, and to overcome the military-industrial power and hubris of Babylon. When true witness is given to this awesome Neighbor, it is about rescue, liberation, and transformation:

> I, I am Yahweh,
>> and besides me there is no savior.
> I declared and saved and proclaimed,
>> when there was no strange god among you
>> and you are my witnesses, says Yahweh.
> I am God, and also henceforth I am He;
>> there is no one who can deliver from my hand;
>> I work and who can hinder it? . . .
> Thus says Yahweh,
>> who makes a way in the sea,
>> a path in the mighty waters,
> who brings out chariot and horse, army and warrior; . . .
> I am about to do a new thing;
>> now it springs forth, do you not perceive it? (Isa 43:11–13, 16–17a, 19a)

The truth about Yahweh is that Yahweh is about to disrupt and make a newness. If Israel tells falsehood about Yahweh, then

Yahweh will be weak, passive, and impotent, yet another adornment of the status quo. This truth or falsehood about this holy, magisterial Neighbor is not a cognitive matter of having the right "idea." It is rather a practical, concrete matter of voicing the authority, energy, and legitimacy of living a liberated life and thereby going home. False or true witness concerns the actual future of life in the world. Those who are "kept" and domesticated by Babylon may lie about Yahweh. Those prepared for Yahweh's alternative future, however, tell the truth which causes the dismantling of the powers of alienation and death, powers which thrive only on falsehood.

Truth-telling about Jesus

When this ancient agrarian prohibition is made larger and more public by the prophets, and then is carried into the New Testament, the requirement of *telling the truth about God* devolves into *telling the truth about Jesus*. The Fourth Gospel, like Deutero-Isaiah, is cast in juridical rhetoric, in order to make an argument and stage a dispute about the true character of Jesus. In this regard, Israel is not to bear false witness against its neighbor, and the church is not to bear false witness against Jesus.[13]

In the Fourth Gospel, John the Baptizer is the forerunner of Jesus to whom witness is first of all made: "You yourselves are my witnesses, that I said, "I am not the Messiah" (John 3:28).

The same rhetoric is employed by Jesus:

> If I testify about myself, my testimony is not true. There is another who testifies on my behalf and I know that his testimony to me is true. You sent messengers to John and he testified to the truth . . . But I have a testimony greater than

---

13. On the importance of juridical language in the Fourth Gospel, see Moss, "The Witnessing Church in the New Testament"; Lincoln, "Trials, Plots and the Narrative of the Fourth Gospel"; and more generally Trites, *New Testament Concept of Witness*, 78–127. Most remarkably, the Fourth Gospel affirms the Paraclete as a witness to Jesus, on which see O'Day's excursus on the Paraclete in "Gospel of John," 774–78.

> John's. The works that the Father has given me to complete,
> the very works I am doing, testify on my behalf that the fa-
> ther has sent me. And the father who sent me has himself
> testified on my behalf. (John 5:31–37)

The Fourth Gospel is presented as a dispute about the truth of Jesus. The assertion and vindication of that truth concerns the character of Jesus, his relation to his Father, and his crucifixion and resurrection.

The Fourth Gospel apparently culminates in the "trial of Jesus," or better, "the trial of Pilate."[14] Before the Roman gover- nor, Jesus asserts: "For this I was born and for this I came into the world, to testify to the truth" (John 18:37). And Pilate hauntingly responds: "What is truth?" (v. 38).

What indeed! The gospel narrative is notoriously enigmatic. But surely it makes a claim, certainly in its own idiom, that in Jesus of Nazareth the things of the world are settled on God's terms. That is the truth before which the Roman governor stands in dismay.

The world—the recalcitrant world presided over by the Ro- man governor—cannot bear the truth of Jesus, for that truth moves beyond our capacity to control and our power to under- stand. And so the world "gives false witness" about Jesus. In doing so, it gives false representation about the world. Just as exilic Jews preferred not to tell the truth about Yahweh because it is a truth too subversive, so many of us in the church choose to bear false witness about Jesus, because the managed, reassuring truth of the empire is more compelling. The truth evidenced in Jesus is not an idea, not a concept, not a formulation, not a fact. It is rather a way of being in the world in suffering and hope, so radical and so raw that we can scarcely entertain it.

Truth-telling about the World

Telling *the truth about God,* telling *the truth about Jesus,* and telling *the truth about the world* are intimately connected to each other.

---

14. On this text, see the helpful comments of O'Day, ibid., 815–27, and the shrewd interpretation by Paul Lehmann in *Transfiguration of Politics,* 48–70.

They are intimately connected in the Sinai covenant whereby God asserts a powerful relation to the world: "It is all mine" (Exod 19:5–6). They are even more visibly linked in the life of Jesus, wherein the purposes of God take fleshly form. Conversely, it is inescapably the case that lying about God, lying about Jesus, and lying about the world are inextricably related to each other.

- We have learned to lie well.[15]

- We imagine that God is not the bestirrer of radical newness.

- We conclude that the suffering of Jesus is not our redemptive vocation.

- We assert that the world—and our economy—is all fine, fine on its own terms with imperial gods and a pliable Jesus.

- We, even with our resolved faith, tend to live inside that reassuring ideology that can recognize nothing deathly and that can receive nothing new.

The world of the Bible consists in a dispute about evidence. The baptized community is "in the dock," summoned to tell the truth and not to bear false witness. The preacher, moreover, is regularly and visibly put on exhibit, to tell the church's truth to the world and to tell God's truth to the church. Very often the world refuses to hear, and of course the church is regularly recalcitrant in receiving testimony. And even the preacher, on occasion, cringes from what must be said, so much are we ourselves accommodated to "the lie."

We can admit all of that. And yet! And yet preaching goes on, folks gather, waiting fearfully but also hopefully for another witness that tells the whole true. And so, good preacher, we may acknowledge the pressure and the way we flinch. But there is also the enduring possibility: Truth in dispute, and our feeble utterance to be sure that our Neighbor is rightly offered and discerned.

The truth now to be told concerns our failed society: "Political power is now firmly in the hands of the money power in a symbiotic relationship that feeds inequity and injustice. Wealth is

---

15. See Peck, *People of the Lie: The Hope for Healing Human Evil.*

derived from power. And power in America is exercised almost exclusively by the wealthy."[16] The prophets know this, and cannot call it "peace." But there is more. The gods of death have pushed hard on Friday. But faithful testimony requires a Sunday "bulletin" that expresses our amazement against the Friday forces of our life.

I am no romantic. I know this explosiveness of Easter that exposes all "prior" truths as false witnesses cannot be said in many churches. The wonder is that it is available to us. It is a truth we not only fear but also crave. Happily some in the church besides us preachers already know. Truth-telling is not easy work. But it is freeing. And it is the only defense the neighborhood has, both our *lowercase "n" neighbors* and our *capital "N" Neighbor.* And we are invited to take no bribes!

16. Goodwin, "A Three-Party Election Won't Address Issue of Economic Injustice."

7

Truth-Telling Comfort

THE EVENTS OF SEPTEMBER 11, 2001 (the airplane hijackings and crashes in New York City; Shanksville, Pennsylvania; and Arlington, Virginia), evoke for me the sobering verdict of Karl Barth:

> As ministers we ought to speak of God. We are human, however, and so cannot speak of God. We ought therefore to recognize both our obligation and our inability and by that very recognition give God the glory.[1]

This surely is the perplexity in which pastors of the church find ourselves always, but intensely so in the face of that ominous happening. Of course I have no warrant to speak beyond that of every sister and brother in ministry to speak when we cannot; but like every brother and sister in ministry, I have some obligation to try.

Grief and Comfort

The first word to be spoken in and by the church of course concerns *grief and comfort* over the insane loss of life that is, in the

---

1. Barth, *The Word of God and the Word of Man,* 186.

countless concrete cases, completely nonsensical. The grief is about loss, more so about meaningless, violent loss, and it must be uttered deep and loud and long, and not quenched soon. I suspect that the church will be driven to texts of sadness such as it has not "needed" for a long time. The grief surely concerns personal loss. For this, a series of lament psalms provide a powerful script.

But the loss, beyond the personal, is a systemic shattering, a new public sense of vulnerability and outrage, an abrupt subverting of our shared sense that we in the United States are somehow immune from the rage of the world. There is currently great attention to "Lament Psalms" as they function in "pastoral care," an immense gain in church practice. Not so much noticed, however, are "communal laments" (such as Psalms 74, 79) that bespeak the shattering of the most elemental public symbols of coherence and meaning, in the Old Testament embodied in the Jerusalem temple. This public dimension of grief is deep underneath personal loss, and for the most part, not easily articulated among us. But grief will not be worked well or adequately until attention goes underneath the personal to the public and communal. My expectation is that pastors, liturgically and pastorally, most need to provide opportunity and script for lament and complaint and grief for a long time. No second maneuver after grief shall be permitted to crowd in upon this raw, elemental requirement.

The full voice of grief is to be matched by the *enactment of comfort* that seeks to meet grief. That comfort begins with bodily contact, but eventually we must speak about the God of all comfort beyond our feeble but indispensable personal offer of comfort. I suspect that in our effort to speak credible comfort, we will be driven back to Easter seriousness, an Easter claim that has not been very serious or even credible in much of our bourgeois self-sufficiency. The claim on which everything rests for us, however, is that the God of the Gospel has rendered impotent "the last enemy" who can no longer rob us of life with the God of whom Paul affirms:

> For I am sure that neither death, nor life, nor angels, nor
> rulers, nor things present, nor things to come, nor powers,

nor height, nor depth, nor anything else in all creation, will
be able to separate us from the love of God in Christ Jesus
our Lord. (Rom 8:38–39)

We pastors utter these words almost every time there is a fu-
neral. But now, I suspect, we will be tested by this required Easter
utterance. On the one hand, we will be tested to see if we subscribe
enough ourselves to say it; on the other, we are challenged to make
sure that the affirmation is not glib in its failure to credit the du-
rability of Friday and the permeability of Saturday, the power of
which is not fully sated by Sunday morning. Church people will be
helped by the affirmation that the anguish of Friday and Saturday
persists, as we know in our own experience.

Grief and comfort come first, and are the peculiar work of the
believing community. For it is the comfort out beyond our management, the reality of God, that makes grief without protective
denial possible. It is now frequently said that the U.S. church is
"theologically soft" on the things that count. Now we shall see. We
shall variously find out for ourselves in the dark silent hours of
pastoral resolve.

The Power of Negation

Beyond that obvious but urgent pastoral task that is entrusted peculiarly to such as us, we are drawn back to first questions by *the
power of negation,* the kind of question that we often need not face.
President Bush has said in response to the disaster, "Our nation
has seen evil." He of course did not exposit his use of the word
"evil"; but his usage has given me pause. Most likely the President
referred to the "evil persons" who committed this act of brutality,
and that dimension of evil is not to be discounted.

But for pastors, the term "evil" evokes more, and is not easily contained in human explanations about particular sins enacted
by human agents. For "evil" draws us beyond "bad deeds" to cosmic questions. Very much Christian triumphalism claims easily
that God in Jesus—at Easter—has eliminated the cosmic power
of negation. Barth, however, has written of the durable power of

"Nothingness," and almost all of us are familiar with Cullmann's suggestive notion about the continued threat of the enemy between "D Day" and "VE Day." More recently, Jon Levenson, a Jewish interpreter, has shown that in the Hebrew Bible evil as a cosmic force persists, made visible in concrete acts but not contained in or reduced to visible acts. Evil persists in a powerful way in defiance of the will of the creator.

So what shall we tell our children? Perhaps we will have learned enough from the Jewish Holocaust to refrain from any glib triumphalism, in order to affirm that God's crucified way in the world continues to be vulnerable and at risk from the demonic forces that may be in a last gasp, but in a powerful last gasp. Our children, so protected and privileged, may need to be delivered from romantic innocence to recognize that we live in a profoundly contested world, contested all the way down between God's good will and the deathliness of evil. Our commitment in the thick contest, moreover, matters, so that when we sign on (in baptism), we join the contest as partisans of the Vulnerable One, and join the at-risk vocation that is the God-willed future of the world.

Self-criticism

Finally, of course, pastors with a cunning sense of good timing will eventually have to raise questions about U.S. policy and U.S. entanglement in the spiral of violence that continues to escalate. Much of popular opinion, reinforced by official posturing, acts as though Reinhold Niebuhr had never spoken about U.S. innocence and self-righteousness. The huge temptation for "Christian America" is to imagine that the U.S. is a righteous empire that endlessly does good around the world, comfortably portrayed in Manichean categories of good and evil.[2] Such knee-jerk response to the crisis traffics in a combination of chauvinism and unreflective Christian triumphalism that refuses to think systemically about the U.S. as

2. Note Reagan's use of "the Evil Empire" for the U.S.S.R.; on American "exceptionalism," see Reinhold Niebuhr, *Moral Man and Immoral Society* and *The Irony of American History*.

the international bully that continues to enact and embody the "Christian West" against non-Christian societies with its huge economic leverage, and with immense, unrivalled military power. And with the gospel of Western globalism, the U.S. is passionately committed to override the fabric of any other kind of culture.

The prophetic task surely has never been more problematic for us than in this issue. The old texts articulate the stunning claim that God can indeed critique and move against God's own chosen people. The simple prophetic articulation by itself is too raw and must be accompanied by patient education in systemic analysis of power, an analysis is known and implied in the prophetic texts, but seldom made explicit.

There will be, to be sure, little patience among us for such systemic analysis, and pastors should not in my judgment, resort to this second task too soon. But if pastors eventually settle only for interpersonal "grief and comfort," the deep issues of U.S. militarism in the service of U.S. consumerism will go unexplored, because there is almost nobody else for such analysis and such utterance.

This is a moment in which pastors, both liberal and conservative, might move out of deathly intramural spats to face big questions about good and evil, and about our U.S. location in the midst of it all. Pastors who face such questions will be engaged in deep questions of their own faith. Pastors who face such questions will be beleaguered, because a triumphant society does not relish truth-telling.

It occurs to me that Paul's lyrical declaration about ministry, so popular in more-or-less innocent ordination sermons, is a moving resource for today:

> We are afflicted in every way, but not crushed;
>> perplexed, but not driven to despair,
>>> persecuted, but not forsaken;
>>>> struck down, but not destroyed;
> always carrying in the body the death of Jesus, so that the life of Jesus may also be made visible in our bodies. (2 Cor 4:8–10)

As you know, Paul concludes: "Therefore we do not lose heart" (v. 16). The heartless evils of September 11 could cause loss of heart. But our heart is set elsewhere in joy and freedom, in grace and in truth-telling about the God of all truth.

I suggest that there are a series of important pastoral tasks concerning *grief comfort, cosmic evil,* and *social analysis.* The evils of yesterday create a new context for preaching. The rawness will make for careful alternative listening, because the word the church has now to speak matters enormously. Having said that, I finish by insisting, yet again, that the first task is grief, grief to be done long and well before anything else (see Rom 3:7; 15:8).

September 12, 2001

8

"Until" . . . Endlessly Enacted, Now Urgent

PSALM 73 STANDS AT the center of the Psalter, the first Psalm of the third "book."[1] It stands, moreover, at the center of the pietistic tradition of faith in which I have been nurtured and in which I gladly stand. I am aware that Psalm 73 does not really fit the theme of this colloquium, but this is my last chance. Besides that, Psalm 73 may be the model for all television commercials that are organized as "before" and "after," so consider this remarkable statement of faith.[2]

---

1. This originated as a sermon preached at the Columbia Theological Seminary Colloquium on "Shaking Earth and Heaven," April 21, 2003. It is offered with special thanks to my colleagues, Beth Johnson and Kathleen M. O'Connor.

2. For further analysis of Psalm 73, see Brueggemann, *Psalms and the Life of Faith*, 203–10; Brueggemann and Miller, "Psalm 73 as a Canonical Marker"; McCann, "Psalm 73: A Microcosm of Old Testament Theology"; Kraus, *Psalms 60–150*, 82–93; Mowinckel, *Psalms in Israel's Worship*, 2:36–39.

God Is Good to Israel

The premise of the psalm in v. 1 is the premise of Old Testament faith, the premise of the faith in which we stand: Truly God is good to Israel. This attestation knows that God is deeply, genuinely, abidingly, reliably committed to God's people. This is the creator God who does good and gives good abundantly. This is the electing God of Exodus who has settled on this community of the beloved. This is the God of wisdom who keeps the world functioning generously. This is the God of whom the church confesses, "That all things work together for good for those who love God who are called according to his purpose" (Rom 8:28).

Scoffing a God Who Watches

But some doubted (Matt 28:17)! Among those who doubted is this psalmist. He did not doubt out of careful reasoning. He simply found another practice of life more attractive and more compelling. He was an Israelite under Torah discipline; when he looked beyond his own rigorous practice, however, he noticed those who held Torah loosely, who got along very well indeed, without all the restraints that he had learned to take as normative. He watched them carefully . . . and envied them:

> For they have no pain;
>> their bodies are sound and sleek.
> They are not in trouble as others are;
>> they are not plagued like other people. (Ps 73:4–5)

They lived very well. They are easy with casual morals; they are not worried about their neighbors; but they go from strength to strength, from party to party, from portfolio to portfolio. And out of that carefree way in the world, they become celebrities:

> Therefore the people turn and praise them,
>> and find no fault in them. (Ps 73:10)

Eventually they are so successful and so full of themselves that they scoff at the notion of a God who watches and monitors and judges. Our speaker noticed them; he disapproved of them; and then he wanted what they wanted. He wanted to be like them! He could not keep his eyes off them. He decided to give up his Torah piety because it wasn't worth it:

> All in vain I have kept my heart clean
>> and washed my hands in innocence.
> For all day long I have been plagued,
>> and am punished every morning. (Ps 73:13–14)

I imagine this psalm to be the voice of a pastor who is required to go to church seven days a week, not treated very well or paid very well, who eventually notices how well off are those who do not live that way, who at least have free weekends! There is an aching ambivalence in this utterance when faith becomes too expensive and other ways tempt and seduce, so that faith relaxes and Torah is compromised.

Perceiving an Unsustainable Life

But then, beginning at v. 18, speaks a second voice in the Psalm, a contrasting voice that comes out of the same mouth. For this psalmist, like all of us, is double-minded and double-tongued. This is the "after" as I have just characterized the "before." Now the psalmist is in a new place. He is a convinced, confirmed child of the covenant, confident of Torah, glad for his identity as a child of God. He now knows, beyond a shadow of a doubt, that the mad pursuit of *commodity* by his consuming neighbors is not all it's cracked up to be. He now knows that the wild life of eager self-indulgence cannot be sustained, and even while it is sustained, it cannot bring joy or well-being. He now knows that easy living without caring much is risky. He had seen the model of life at ease and with no pain. But now, on second thought,

> Truly you set them in slippery places;
>
>> you make them fall to ruin.
>
> How they are destroyed in a moment,
>
>> swept away utterly by terrors! (Ps 73:18–20)

Such a life has no staying power, no gravitas, no quality of existence that one would finally envy. Such a life is a fantasy created by image-makers who readily dupe naive Torah-keepers. It cannot be sustained!

So he says, I woke up to reality, and discovered that I had been a real jerk to be attracted to that way of life. Well, not a jerk, but a "brute beast," stupid and ignorant. This psalmist reviews the slippery slope he had gone down but had stopped before his life was completely shattered, just in the nick of time.

As a rhetorical trigger concerning that other way that he now dismisses as phony, he utters his great evangelical "nevertheless":

> *Nevertheless* I am continually with you;
>
>> you hold my right hand.
>
> You guide me with your counsel,
>
>> and afterward you will receive me with honor. (Ps 73:23–24)

The psalmist has come to the judgment that while the others are in slippery places his right hand is held by God, the God of Torah, so that he cannot slip. He now knows that this God is an adequate guide, quite in contrast to those who are sadly and destructively misguided. And then he arrives at one of the most eloquent statements of faith in all of our tradition:

> Whom have I in heaven but you?
>
>> And there is nothing on earth that I desire other than you.
>
> My flesh and my heart may fail,
>
>> but God is the strength of my heart and my portion forever.
>
> (Ps 73:25–26)

Whom indeed in heaven but you: *No one!* What on earth, but you: *Nothing! Only you,* only this God as the source and center and clue to life. He says, "God is my portion," and "portion" here means property, estate, entitlement. The speaker is clearly willing to forego all of the *commodities* of his seductive neighbors for the sake of this *communion* that is the complete fulfillment of his destiny.

His conclusion is that the very best thing is to be near God who is safe refuge and utter guarantee. The contrast between communion with God and that other tempting way of life is total and unqualified. And so, like Israel frequently does, the Psalm ends in praise:

> I have made the Lord GOD my refuge,
>> to tell of all your works. (Ps 73:28b)

Getting from Commodity to Communion

This psalm is a rather naive statement of the seductions and settlements of faith. It states a single either/or of *commodity* or *communion* and comes down on the side of the covenant. It echoes, surely, the teaching of Deuteronomy about the way of life and the way of death, always a chance, always a decision, and here is a model articulation of faith well embraced.

What should interest us, I imagine, is how to get from *commodity* to *communion,* for it is a travail that we and our children and our grandchildren face. Clearly our nation has become a market in which everything and everyone is reduced to a tradable commodity, and now a market embedded in an empire. It is primarily the ones "without pain" who "increase in riches" who are the war planners and the stockholders and the decision-makers—and all of us who invest in imperial "growth." Clearly the church is tempted to transpose its practice of good news in order to compete for a share of the market. And who among us does not have the simplicity of our faith made seductively complex by attractions that are shrill and loud and constant, promises of well-being and comfort and communion without the shadow of the cruciform entering in? My judgment is that the travail of the psalmist is not remote from the church, its practices, its pastors and its would-be pastors, not distant from many men and women and children who name the name, that name being enmeshed so powerfully now in a commodity enterprise.

Turning Point

At the center, the psalmist tells us how he moved from seduction to confidence, from commodity to communion. It was not an easy move:

> But when I thought how to understand this,
> > it seemed to me a wearisome task. (Ps 73:16)

It was, however, a move he made:

> until I went into the sanctuary of God;
> > then I perceived their end. (Ps 73:17)

This is the big *until* that breaks the spell of consumer ideology. This is the barbed rhetorical inconvenience that questions the magic of the market and is supportive military apparatus. This "until" is the big, jarring disruption that makes alternative life possible. "Until I went to the sanctuary." Maybe he went out of habit: "I was glad when they said unto me . . ." But even if out of habit, this time there was a seriousness and an urgency, a wondering and a receptiveness. When he was there, in any case, it all became clear. Perhaps he was long nurtured to be ready for this flash of understanding. Or perhaps it was an abrupt new claim that came to him right out of God's holiness. In any case, the speaker arrives at a deeply new orientation. The psalmist does not tell how it happened:

- Maybe it was a mystical visionary encounter like that of Isaiah in the year that King Uzziah died (Isaiah 6). Maybe.

- But the custodian had noticed, in 1 Kgs 8:9, that there was no "presence" in the ark, only two tablets of Torah. So perhaps the "until" was only a new hearing of the commandments he had heard long ago in his family. The psalmist does not tell us, but he comes away from that moment focused and grounded and no longer captive to the slickness of the alternative.

- Or if we transpose the "until" into Christian parlance, it is "until" . . . "the word became flesh and lived among us, and we have seen his glory, the glory as of a father's only son, full of grace and truth" (John 1:14).

We have looked into the face of Jesus and have seen the ultimate offer of communion, grace and truth, generosity and reliability that the cheap self-indulgence of the community around cannot make on its way to death.

Either way:

—*until* a vision of God in the temple, or

—*until* a re-entry into the commandments, or

—*until* seeing the face of the crucified . . .

Either way . . . until I went into the sanctuary and perceived their latter end.

The Prodigal Son

At the core of our faith is a gift to be received, a gift to be received in an upstream decision that contradicts the easier decisions of our culture. I judge that the church in the U.S.—in a market-driven, war-hungering, empire-thirsting environment—is at the brink of a great "until" that lets us see that the promises of this deathly ideology are indeed deathly promises, and that the alternative is the one who is endlessly our true home, our best portion, and our deep desire.

I mention now Jesus' parable of the Prodigal.[3] It occurred to me that this story is Jesus' midrashic commentary on Psalm 73

---

3. For further analyses of the Prodigal story, see Scott, *Hear Then the Parable*, 99–126; and Malina and Rohrbaugh, *Social-Science Commentary on the Synoptic Gospels*, 288–91.

in which the son plays the role of the psalmist. He is, "before," a practitioner of commodity:

> Then Jesus said, "There was a man who had two sons. The younger of them said to his father, 'Father, give me the share of the property that will belong to me.'" So he divided his property between them. (Luke 15:11–12)

And he ends that scenario in a failed pursuit:

> When he had spent everything, a severe famine took place throughout that country, and he began to be in need. So he went and hired himself out to one of the citizens of that country, who sent him to his fields to feed the pigs. He would gladly have filled himself with the pods that the pigs were eating; and no one gave him anything. (15:14–16)

Then we are witnesses to his "after" when he returns home:

> So he set off and went to his father. But while he was still far off, his father saw him and was filled with compassion; he ran and put his arms around him and kissed him. Then the son said to him, "Father, I have sinned against heaven and before you; I am no longer worthy to be called your son." But the father said to his slaves, "Quickly, bring out a robe—the best one—and put it on him; put a ring on his finger and sandals on his feet. And get the fatted calf and kill it, and let us eat and celebrate; for this son of mine was dead and is alive again; he was lost and is found!" And they began to celebrate. (15:20–24)

He now is a celebrated child of the household and has come to the place where he ought to be.

But what interests us is the hidden turn of the narrative that is reported—like in Psalm 73—but also like Psalm 73, not described: When he came to himself (15:17).

What an incredible phrase! We do not know how that happened, anymore than we know how the "until" in the Psalm worked. The teller of the story might have said, "Until he came to himself," because it is the same "until."

But, of course, the son does not just come "to himself." He comes to "himself" in his true identity. He comes to *himself as a beloved son* of the father. He in fact comes in his "until" to recognize that his father was the only one he wanted to be with:

> Whom have I in heaven but you?
>> And there is nothing on earth that I desire other than you.
> My flesh and my heart may fail,
>> but God is the strength of my heart and my portion forever.
>
> (Ps 73:25–26)

It did not matter anymore to this son that his older brother got the farm as his "portion," because the father is the son's "portion," and the only thing he wants in heaven or on earth. The son "coming to himself is a decision grounded in the father's love that permits him to slough off his false self and become finally who he is. It is clear that in this telling that Jesus fully understood the psalm. Indeed, Jesus' engagement in ministry is, among other things, that we should be weaned from the seductions of *commodity* for the gift of *communion,* a presence that leaves us in joy and well-being.

Such a poem of piety as this psalm is of course remote from our concern with the emerging world order in all of its rich complexity. Except that it is worth noting that the surge of "globalization" that besets the world church is indeed a pursuit of commodity, an overriding of local cultures in the interest of market control, and the necessary support of militarism. The world writ large is caught, as was our psalmist, as was the wayward son, in a death script. The news is that it need not be so. The news is that a powerful "until" can lead to a buoyant "nevertheless." The church, in all the complexities of globalization—and now imperialism— knows about this modest "until" and knows that everything depends upon it. Imagine that the church is the carrier of this "until" that permits well-being while the way of death and all of its terrors vanish like a phantom. We are "until" people with much to decide because we know about the "after" of life with God, our heart's true home.

Bibliography

Achtemeier, Elizabeth. *The Community and Message of Isaiah 56–66.* Minneapolis: Augsburg, 1982.

Albertz, Rainer. *A History of Israelite Religion in the Old Testament Period.* 2 vols. Translated by John Bowden. OTL. Louisville: Westminster John Knox, 1994.

———. *Persönliche Frömmigkeit und offizielle Religion.* Calwer Theologische Monographien 9. Stuttgart: Calwer Verlag, 1978.

Alt, Albrecht. "Micah 2:1–5." In *Kleine Schriften*, vol. 3, 373–81. Munich: Beck, 1959.

———. "Das Verbot des Diebstahls im Dekalog." In *Kleine Schriften*, vol. 1, 333–40. Munich: Beck, 1955.

Anderson, Bernhard W. "Exodus and Covenant in Second Isaiah and Prophetic Tradition." In *Magnalia Dei: The Mighty Acts of God,* edited by Frank Moore Cross et al., 339–60. Garden City, NY: Doubleday, 1976.

———. "Exodus Typology in Second Isaiah." In *Israel's Prophetic Heritage,* edited by Bernhard W. Anderson and Walter Harrelson, 177–95. New York: Harper & Row, 1962.

Augustine. *The Confessions of St Augustine, Bishop of Hippo.* Translated by E. B. Pusey. New York: Dutton, 1950.

Barth, Karl. *Church Dogmatics,* Vol. 3.3: *The Doctrine of Creation.* Translated by Geoffrey W. Bromiley et al. Edinburgh: T. & T. Clark, 1960.

———. *The Word of God and the Word of Man.* Translated with a new Foreword by Douglas Horton. New York: Harper, 1957.

Bellah, Robert, et al. *Habits of the Heart: Individualism and Commitment in American Life.* Berkeley: University of California Press, 1985.

Berger, Peter, Brigitte Berger, and Hansfried Kellner, *The Homeless Mind.* New York: Random House, 1973.

Bollas, Christopher. *The Shadow of the Object: Psychoanalysis of the Unthought Known*. New York: Columbia University Press, 1987.

Brown, William P., editor. *The Ten Commandments: The Reciprocity of Faithfulness*. Library of Theological Ethics. Louisville: Westminster John Knox, 2004.

Brueggemann, Walter. "The Book of Exodus." In *New Interpreters Bible*, vol. 1, 675–981. Nashville: Abingdon, 1994.

———. *Finally Comes the Poet: Daring Speech for Proclamation*. Minneapolis: Fortress, 1989.

———. *Hopeful Imagination: Prophetic Voices in Exile*. Philadelphia: Fortress, 1986.

———. *The Message of the Psalms: A Theological Commentary*. Augsburg Old Testament Studies. Minneapolis: Augsburg, 1984.

———. *Praying the Psalms: Engaging Scripture and the Life of the Spirit*. 2nd ed. Eugene, OR: Cascade Books, 2007.

———. *The Prophetic Imagination*. 2nd ed. Minneapolis: Fortress, 2001.

———. *The Psalms and the Life of Faith*. Edited by Patrick D. Miller. Minneapolis: Fortress, 1995.

Brueggemann, Walter, and Patrick D. Miller. "Psalm 73: as a Canonical Marker." *Journal for the Study of the Old Testament* 72 (1996) 45–56.

Buber, Martin. *The Kingship of God*. Translated by Richard Scheimann. New York: Harper & Row, 1967.

———. *The Prophetic Faith*. Translated by Carlyle Witton-Davies. New York: Harper & Row, 1949.

———. *Tales of the Hasidim: The Early Masters*. Translated by Olga Marx. New York: Schocken, 1947.

Busch, Eberhard. *Karl Barth: His Life from Letters and Autobiographical Texts*. 1976. Reprinted, Eugene, OR: Wipf & Stock, 2005.

Calvin, John. *Commentary on the Book of Psalms, Volume Second*. Grand Rapids: Baker, 1979.

Chaney, Marvin L. "You Shall Not Covet Your Neighbor's House." *Pacific Theological Review* 15 (Winter 1982) 3–13. Reprinted in *The Ten Commandments: The Reciprocity of Faithfulness*, edited by William P. Brown, 302–18. Library of Theological Ethics. Louisville: Westminster John Knox, 2004.

Childs, Brevard S. *Biblical Theology of the Old and New Testaments: Theological Reflection on the Christian Bible*. Minneapolis: Fortress, 1992.

———. *The Book of Exodus*. Old Testament Library. Philadelphia: Westminster, 1974.

———. *Old Testament Theology in a Canonical Context*. Philadelphia: Fortress, 1985.

Chomsky, Noam. *Necessary Illusions: Thought Control in Democratic Societies.* Boston: South End, 1989.

———. *The Washington Connection and Third World Fascism.* Boston: South End, 1979.

———. *What Uncle Sam Really Wants.* Tucson, AZ: Odonian, 1992.

Crenshaw, James L. *Prophetic Conflict: Its Effect upon Israelite Religion.* BZAW 124. Berlin: de Gruyter, 1971.

Culley, Robert C. *Studies in the Structure of Hebrew Narrative.* Semeia Supplements. Philadelphia: Fortress, 1976.

Dahlberg, Bruce. "On Recognizing the Unity of Genesis." *Theology Digest* 24 (1976) 360–67.

Daube, David. *The Exodus Pattern in the Bible.* London: Faber & Faber, 1963.

Dawn, Marva J. *Sexual Character: Beyond Technique to Intimacy.* Grand Rapids: Eerdmans, 1991.

Duchrow, Ulrich. *Global Economy: A Confessional Issue for the Churches.* Geneva: WCC Publications, 1987.

Eichrodt, Walther. "The Holy One in Your Midst: The Theology of Hosea." *Interpretation* 15 (1961) 259–73.

Ellul, Jacques. *The Humiliation of the Word.* Grand Rapids: Eerdmans, 1991.

———. *Propaganda: The Formation of Men's Attitudes.* New York: Random House, 1973.

———. *Technological Society.* New York: Random House, 1967.

Fackenheim, Emil L. *God's Presence in History: Jewish Affirmations and Philosophical Reflections.* New York: New York University Press, 1970.

Freedman, David Noel. "Divine Commitment and Human Obligation: The Covenant Theme." *Interpretation* 18 (1964) 419–31.

Fretheim, Terrence E. *Exodus.* Interpretation. Louisville: John Knox, 1991.

Galbraith, John Kenneth. *The Culture of Contentment.* Boston: Houghton Mifflin, 1992.

Gnuse, Robert. *You Shall Not Steal: Community and Property in the Biblical Tradition.* Maryknoll, NY: Orbis, 1985.

Goodwin, Richard N. "A Three-Party Election Won't Address Issue of Economic Injustice." *Boston Globe,* Friday, 26 July 1996, A17.

Gottwald, Norman K. *The Tribes of Yahweh: A Sociology of the Religion of Liberated Israel, 1250–1050 BCE.* Maryknoll, NY: Orbis, 1979.

Green, Thomas F. *Voices: The Educational Formation of Conscience.* Notre Dame: University of Notre Dame Press, 1999.

Gunton, Colin. *Enlightenment & Alienation: An Essay Towards a Trinitarian Theology.* Grand Rapids: Eerdmans, 1985.

———. *The One, The Three, and The Many: God, Creation, and the Culture of Modernity.* Cambridge: Cambridge University Press, 1993.

Hall, Douglas John. *Imaging God: Dominion as Stewardship*. Grand Rapids: Eerdmans, 1986.

Hamilton, Jeffries M. *Social Justice and Deuteronomy: The Case of Deuteronomy 15*. SBL Dissertation Series 136. Atlanta: Scholars, 1992.

Hanson, K. C. "'How Honorable!' 'How Shameful!': A Cultural Reading of Analysis of Matthew's Makarisms and Reproaches." *Semeia* 68 (1994[96]) 81–111.

Harrelson, Walter. *The Ten Commandments and Human Rights*. Overtures to Biblical Theology. Philadelphia: Fortress, 1980.

Harris, J. Gordon. *Biblical Perspectives on Aging: God and the Elderly*. Overtures to Biblical Theology. Philadelphia: Fortress, 1987.

Hazard, Paul. *The European Mind, 1680–1715*. New York: World, 1963.

Heschel, Abraham Joshua. *The Sabbath: Its Meaning for Modern Man*. New York: Farrar, Straus, & Young, 1951.

———. *Who is Man?* Stanford: Stanford University Press, 1965.

Jewett, Robert. *Romans: A Commentary*. Hermeneia. Minneapolis: Fortress, 2007.

Käsemann, Ernst. *A Commentary on Romans*. Translated by Geoffrey W. Bromiley. Grand Rapids: Eerdmans, 1980.

Kraus, Hans-Joachim. *Psalms 60–150: A Commentary*. Translated by Hilton C. Oswald. Minneapolis: Augsburg, 1989.

Kutsch, Ernst. "Gesetz und Gnade: Probleme des alttestamentlichen Bundesbegriffs." *Zeitschrift für die alttestamentliche Wissenschaft* 79 (1967) 18–35.

Lang, Bernhard. "The Social Organization of Peasant Poverty in Biblical Israel." *JSOT* 24 (1982) 47–63. Reprinted in *Monotheism and the Prophetic Minority: An Essay in Biblical History and Sociology*, 114–27. Social World of Biblical Antiquity 1. Sheffield, UK: Almond, 1983.

Lehmann, Paul. *The Decalogue and a Human Future: The Meaning of the Commandments for Making and Keeping Human Life Human*. Grand Rapids: Eerdmans, 1994.

———. *The Transfiguration of Politics*. New York: Harper & Row, 1975.

Levenson, Jon D. *Sinai and Zion: An Entry Into the Jewish Bible*. New York: Winston, 1985.

Lifton, Robert J. *The Nazi Doctors: Medical Killing and the Psychology of Genocide*. New York: Basic Books, 1986.

Lincoln, Andrew T. "Trials, Plots and the Narrative of the Fourth Gospel." *JSNT* 56 (1994) 3–30.

Malina, Bruce J., and Richard L. Rohrbaugh. *Social-Science Commentary on the Synoptic Gospels*. 2nd ed. Minneapolis: Fortress, 2003.

Masters, William H., and Virginia E. Johnson. *The Pleasure Bond: A New Look at Sexuality and Commitment.* Boston: Little, Brown, 1974.

McCann, J. Clinton. "Psalm 73: Microcosm of Old Testament Theology." In *The Listening Heart,* edited by Kenneth Hoglund, 247–57. JSOT Supplements 58. Sheffield, UK: JSOT Press, 1987.

McHugh, Paul R. "Psychiatric Misadventures." In *The Best American Essays 1993,* edited by Joseph Epstein, 188–91. New York Ticknor & Fields, 1993.

Mendenhall, George E. *Law and Covenant in Israel and the Ancient Near East.* Pittsburgh: Biblical Colloquium, 1955.

Miles, Margaret R. *Desire and Delight: A New Reading of Augustine's Confessions.* 1992. Reprinted, Eugene, OR: Wipf & Stock, 2006.

Miller, Patrick D. Jr. "The Human Sabbath: A Study in Deuteronomic Theology." *Princeton Seminary Bulletin* 6 (1985) 81–97.

Moran, William L. "The Ancient Near Eastern Background of the Love of God in Deuteronomy." *Catholic Biblical Quarterly* 25 (1963) 77–87.

Moss, Robert V. "The Witnessing Church in the New Testament." *Theology and Life* 3 (1960) 262–68.

Mottus, Henri. "Jeremiah vs. Hananiah: Ideology and Truth in Old Testament Prophecy." In *The Bible and Liberation: Political and Social Hermeneutics,* edited by Norman K. Gottwald, 235–51. Maryknoll, NY: Orbis, 1983.

Mowinckel, Sigmund. *The Psalms in Israel's Worship.* 2 vols. Translated by D. R. Ap-Thomas. 1962. Reprinted, Grand Rapids: Eerdmans, 2004.

Muilenburg, James. *The Way of Israel Biblical Faith and Ethics.* New York: Harper, 1961.

Niebuhr, Reinhold. *The Irony of American History.* New York: Scribners, 1952.
——. *Moral Man and Immoral Society.* 1960. Reprint, with Introduction by Langdon B. Gilkey. Library of Theological Ethics. Louisville: Westminster John Knox, 2001.

Niebuhr, Richard R. *Resurrection and Historical Reason: A Study of Theological Method.* New York: Scribner, 1957.

Nygren, Anders. *Agape and Eros.* Translated by Philip S. Watson. Philadelphia: Westminster, 1953.

O'Day, Gail R. "The Gospel of John." In *New Interpreter's Bible,* vol. 9, 774–78. Nashville: Abingdon, 1995.
——. "Singing Woman's Song: A Hermeneutic of Liberation." *Currents in Theology and Mission* 12 (1985) 203–10.

Overholt, Thomas W. *The Threat of Falsehood: A Study in the Theology of the Book of Jeremiah.* Studies in Biblical Theology 2/16. London: SCM, 1970.

Peck, M. Scott. *People of the Lie: The Hope for Healing Human Evil.* New York: Simon & Schuster, 1985.

Bibliography

Plaut, W. Gunter, "The Sabbath as Protest: Thoughts on Work and Leisure in the Automated Society." In *Tradition and Change in Jewish Experience*, edited by A. Leland Jamison, 169–78. Syracuse, NY: Dept. of Religion, Syracuse University, 1978.

Postman, Neil. *Amusing Ourselves to Death: Public Discourse in the Age of Show Business*. New York: Penguin, 1986.

———. *How to Watch TV News*. New York: Viking Penguin, 1992.

———. *Technopoly: The Surrender of Culture to Technology*. New York: Random House, 1993.

Preuss, Horst Dietrich. *Old Testament Theology*. Vol. 1. Old Testament Library. Louisville: Westminster John Knox, 1995.

Rad, Gerhard von. "Brother and Neighbor in the Old Testament." In *God at Work in Israel*, 183–93. Translated by John H. Marks. Nashville Abingdon, 1980.

———. *Moses*. 2nd ed. Translated by Stephen Neill. Foreword by Walter Brueggemann. Edited by K. C. Hanson. Eugene, OR: Cascade Books, 2011.

Richard, Pablo, editor. *The Idols of Death and the God of Life: A Theology*. Translated by Barbara E. Campbell and Bonnie Shepard. Maryknoll, NY: Orbis, 1983.

Sanders, E. P. *Paul and Palestinian Judaism: A Comparison of Patterns of Religion*. Philadelphia: Fortress, 1977.

Sanders, James A. "Canonical Hermeneutics: True and False Prophecy." In *From Sacred Story to Sacred Text*, 87–105. Philadelphia: Fortress, 1987.

Schmid, Hans Heinrich. "Rechtfertigung als Schöpfungsgeschehen." In *Rechtfertigung: Festschrift für Ernst Käsemann zum 70. Geburtstag*, edited by Johannes Friedrich, Wolfgang Pöhlmann, and Peter Stuhlmacher, 403–14. Göttingen: Vandenhoeck & Ruprecht, 1976.

Scott, Bernard Brandon. *Hear Then the Parable: A Commentary on the Parables of Jesus*. Minneapolis: Fortress, 1989.

Soelle, Dorothee. *Beyond Mere Obedience*. Translated by Lawrence W. Denef. Minneapolis: Augsburg, 1970.

Stendahl, Krister. "The Apostle Paul and the Introspective Conscience of the West." In *Paul among Jews and Gentiles and Other Essays*, 78–96. Philadelphia: Fortress, 1976.

Teilhard de Chardin, Pierre. *Building the Earth*. Translated by Noël Lindsay. Wilkes-Barre, PA: Dimension Books, 1965.

Terrien, Samuel. *The Elusive Presence: Toward a New Biblical Theology*. 1978. Reprinted, Eugene, OR: Wipf & Stock, 2000.

Tracy, David. *The Analogical Imagination*. New York: Crossroad, 1981.

Trites, Allison A. *The New Testament Concept of Witness*. Society for New Testament Studies Monograph Series 31. Cambridge: Cambridge University Press, 1977.

Tsevat, Matitiahu. "The Basic Meaning of the Biblical Sabbath." In *The Meaning of the Book of Job and Other Biblical Studies: Essays on the Literature and Religion of the Hebrew Bible*. New York: Ktav, 1980.

Van Buren, Paul M. *Discerning the Way: A Theology of the Jewish Christian Reality*. New York: Seabury, 1980.

———. *A Theology of the Jewish Christian Reality, Part 2: A Christian Theology of the People Israel*. San Francisco: Harper & Row, 1987.

Via, Dan O. Jr. *Kerygma and Comedy in the New Testament*. Philadelphia: Fortress, 1975.

Walzer, Michael. *Exodus and Revolution*. New York: Basic Books, 1985.

Wilder, Amos Niven. *Theopoetic: Theology and the Religious Imagination*. Philadelphia: Fortress, 1976.

Willimon, William H. *Peculiar Speech: Preaching to the Baptized*. Grand Rapid: Eerdmans, 1992.

Wolff, Hans Walter. *The Anthropology of the Old Testament*. Translated by Margaret Kohl. Philadelphia: Fortress, 1974.

———. "Micah the Moreshite—The Prophet and His Background." In *Israelite Wisdom: Theological and Literary Essays in Honor of Samuel Terrien*, edited by John G. Gammie et al., 77–84. Homage Series 3. Missoula, MT: Scholars, 1978.

Wright, N. T. *Jesus and the Victory of God*. The New Testament and the People of God 2. Minneapolis: Fortress, 1996.

Wrong, Dennis H. *The Problem of Order: What Unites and Divides Society*. New York: Free Press, 1994.

Yankelovitch, Daniel. *New Rules: Searching for Self-Fulfillment in a World Turned Upside Down*. New York: Bantam, 1982.

Index of Scripture

Index of Names